1988

GW00836482

Hungry for the West

Edited by David Foot

REDCLIFFE
Bristol

First published in 1988
by Redcliffe Press Ltd.,
49 Park St., Bristol.

© David Foot

ISBN 0 948265 57 4

The main text in this book
has been set in Baskerville 11/12pt
Roman to a measure of 26 ems

Typesetting and printing by
WBC Print, Bristol

Contents

Acknowledgements

This publication is a tribute to all who, between the wars, put on the gloves – and we thank especially those we have interviewed in the compilation of this book. We leaned on the enthusiasm, help and knowledge of local boxing's own historian Jack Phelps and we are grateful to him.

We thank those who offered valuable encouragement in the preparation of the book. They were

HTV   Clifford Hill
Courage Ltd   Bert Nutt
Ray Purnell (Bristol Exhibition Centre)   John Newth

Photographs of Jack Phelps (with his gloves and seated with the boy boxers) were taken by John Stubbs. A number of the modern photographs of old-time boxers and of old locations were taken by Mark Foot. We are grateful to them and also thank the following for the kind loan of pictures: Jack Phelps, the families of the late Bert Budd and Benny McNeill, Terry Harding, Bert Nutt, Reg Hobbs, Len Munden, Tommy Bartlett, Arnold Rose and B.U.P.

Benny McNeill, who came from Fishponds, Bristol was without question one of the West's most colourful boxers — and certainly among the unluckiest. He fought extensively in America and on the continent and earned big money. But he lost most of it, the victim of exploitation, too many cadging hangers-on and because of his own generosity. In his hey-day, he stayed in the best American hotels, met Charlie Chaplin and was proud of the fact that he gave Gene Tunney some early tuition. Featherweight Benny had an attractive style in the ring. He gained verdicts over Kid Williams, the American bantamweight champion, and himself held the inter-armies bantamweight and lightweight titles during the First World War. Well known for his courage, he once insisted on fighting despite an attack of double-pneumonia, and collapsed in the 11th round. Benny went to prison on a manslaughter charge after attacking a relative. But his four children are convinced he was provoked and unfairly punished. He was described as a good, kind, placid father who enjoyed gardening and encouraging young boxers at his Knowle home. Here he is shown in the impressive headwear, as he appeared at an American theatre where he was making a personal appearance. Benny died in 1953.

4

Introduction

This is a book essentially about those West Country boxers, many of them from the Bristol area, who fought professionally — usually for a few pounds — in the years between the two great wars. It is important to put their words and their experiences on record as a piece of social history. In some cases they fought so that there could be food on the table at home. Apart from being an account of exhilarating bouts in improvised boxing rings and romantically remembered halls, once heavy with Woodbine smoke and throbbing collective excitement, this is a story of marvellous, warm-hearted characters who emerged from the grey working-class ghettos of a city where the dole queues were long and the faces carried the bleak, helpless looks of the times.

For scores of wan and wiry boys and young men, boxing provided an elusive whiff of glamour. They crowded into the little gyms dotted around Bedminster and east Bristol. They saved their pennies to go to the regular small-time promotions. They created their own heroes, following them week after week from one bout to the next.

Many of the fighters doubled-up on the booths or "the sloggers" as they were known. It was a valuable training ground and a source of additional income in the summer months. The public listened to the showmen's spiel, enjoyed the raucous build-up and didn't often complain about the "plants" in the crowd or the fact that there was often a good-natured deception about the whole thing.

Booths were an exciting and colourful feature of local fairs. Just occasionally the atmosphere could turn unpleasant and one or two incidents are related, at first hand, in this book. There was the night at Horfield Common where an ex-sailor, his strength and brash claims fortified by a prolonged visit to the Wellington, boastfully challenged Jimmy Jury. "Teach him a lesson, Jimmy," was the booth advice.

The bout lasted for two eventful rounds. There were plenty of blows exchanged. Then the capable Jimmy, who used to lodge in St. Michael's Hill, hit the challenger flush on the jaw. Down went his opponent, out cold. He was carried outside and laid on the grass. His wife was there in tears and his two children peered down, equally apprehensive. A recent tragedy in a booth contest elsewhere added unease to the moment. Eventually the one-time sailor regained consciousness and staggered off, a few compensatory pence in his pocket. Jimmy, relieved like the rest of the retinue, pulled on his gloves again and went back onto the stand, ready for the next fight. Booth boxing could be crude — and it wasn't for the squeamish.

As for the official boxing shows, in converted picture palaces and swimming baths as well as Old Market halls and the beloved Arcade Hall at Bedminster, they were enthusiastically organised. But they sometimes lacked finesse and many of the safeguards that later became compulsory.

Bristol was no different from many other centres in those down-to-earth days when rules were known to be bent if not broken outright. Much winking went on. Matchmaking could be a mockery with minimal regard to a boxer's weight, whatever the official announcement implied. Medical supervision wasn't always guaranteed. "What's the matter, old son? I've got some sticking plaster in me trouser pocket, han't I?'

Gum shields weren't necessarily in evidence. Some of the lads climbed through the ropes with faded old overcoats across their shoulders; they hadn't graduated to dressing gowns. A few of the fights may have been fixed — but not many. It wasn't worth it when there was so little at stake.

The youngsters from the slums of Bristol had little work. But church and youth organisations encouraged them to keep fit and look after their bodies. Physical culture was advertised in the papers. There was a certain working class status in putting on the gloves. The Dockland Settlement and the Barton Hill Boxing Club reverberated each night with the thud of glove on punchbag.

Bert Budd was fostering an interest in the sport at The Crown, Lawford's Gate, with his well-equipped St. Jude's Club, and elsewhere. Earlier there had been Charlie Hobbs at the Beer Cask in Pennywell Road and Bert Wakefield (Drill Hall, Old Market) among others. It was better than fighting in the streets or in the sawdust pubs that dotted St. Paul's, St. Jude's and St. Agnes. The police looked on approvingly.

The tradition of boxing in the area was authentic enough. This was where the bareknuckle champions came from. Jem Belcher was one of the first, a title holder in 1800 before he was 20. They called him Napoleon. He lost an eye in an accident away from the ring but still went on fighting those interminable contests.

He lost his heavyweight title in 1805 to another Bristol man, "Game Chicken" Henry Pearce. Here was another great slugger, much loved by the Fancy who feted him at the Hatchet where they placed their bets. "The Game Chicken" derived from "Hen" — and that from Henry. He successfully went 64 rounds with John Gully, an

6

Could popular Freddie Mills, a one-time booth boxer, be sharing a joke about Jimmy Jury's experiences on Horfield Common?

Len Harvey was paid in £1 notes after topping the bill at Eastville.

extraordinary and flamboyant boxer. This son of a Wick butcher was another magnificent, almost surreal character. Not content to be a champion, he went on to become a wealthy landowner and Member of Parliament. Twice he was the owner of the Derby winner.

And then there was Tom Cribb, himself the champion for nine years and beaten only once. This former coal miner with the perfect physique was always a favourite, especially at St. James' fairground in Bristol or at Lansdown, Bath. Lord Byron used to watch him train and immortalised him in verse; the deeds of yet another local boxer, Bill Neate can be found in the published work of William Hazlitt. Bristol journalist Jim Brady has admirably captured the eccentricities and the raw flavour of the period in his book *Strange Encounters*.

We come to the 20th century and we think of more local folk heroes like Chaffey Hayman and "Pudding" Baker the barber, whose wife kept the General Elliott pub, where Jimmy Driscott used to stay while he was training in Bristol at the Lord Nelson. There was heavyweight Mike Flynn and the faggot-and-peas star Harry Mansfield. How we should have liked to see Harry stylishly in action — and Alf Avent, the Bedminster boy who became the amateur bantam weight champion.

Tex O'Rourke, a former American heavyweight turned business-man, came to Bristol in 1923 on behalf of several millionaires, to search optimistically "for a future heavyweight star". He advertised — and sixty aspiring champions around the country turned up for an interview if not quite an audition. At the Royal Hotel, he told Leslie Price and Walker Macron, both from Bristol, a police constable and the son of a hotel proprietor, that they had the right physique and he was prepared to take a chance with them. Sadly it was an American dream that backfired.

The boxing shows multiplied — and so did the characters. How about Eric Chester, "the Gentleman Boxer" as he was sometimes dubbed when he appeared at the Arcade? Eric was full of charm and good manners (despite a rather fearsome right hand) and was known to ask for his opponent's autograph before the fight started. But he got beaten three times on points by Alfie McGill, the one-time milkman and naval petty officer, a likeable, modest man who later became the landlord of the King David Hotel at the bottom of St. Michael's Hill.

Jack Phelps looked after and was often full of praise for "the classy Freddie Gaydon", who had two cauliflower ears ("I couldn't stand the wind on my ears, Jack") and was one of the first local boxers to run his own motor car. In quick succession, at the Arcade, he KO'd Inch Jones, Alf Tite and Pat Patterson. Freddie was later a boxing instructor at Clifton College, where the tradition has gone right through, of course, to recently retired Gordon Hazell.

Bert Budd, 3rd left, keeps a paternal eye on his stable of keen young boxers at his St Jude's Club.

Characters? Where do we start? Big Sam Moore, who used to work at the docks, and as a bookmaker... Billy "Scrammy" Stevens, who worked Alf Cooper's booth... miner's son Roy Locke — good enough to beat Reggie Hall, the local flyweight champ — who later became a window dresser for a brandy firm... Billy Wagner, Tom Ind... debonair Inch Jones, the knock-out specialist from St. Philip's who claimed to be the only one to put Tosh Parker on his back... Tosh himself. And "Soldier". And, we might say, "Sailor" for the bighearted Pat Patterson's ship was torpedoed. Jack Phelps once went home, by the way, with soldier Bradbury's false teeth in his pocket— he'd been handed them for safe keeping, and gave them back 24 hours later.

Most of them were, in their various ways, engaging personalities. One heard Billy Symes, who grew up in a St. Jude's pub, described as "one of the nicest men around". He topped the bill against Tommy Bartlett at the Shepherds Hall, Old Market over eight rounds — and came away with a surprise win. Tommy had won his previous 14 fights. They used to say Billy was just as happy, in his easy-going way, playing snooker or local soccer. But then few could get past Tommy when it was a key match in the Downs League. While we talk of characters, who will forget the Dutchman Robert Disch, who lost to Boyo Rees over 15 rounds at the Colston Hall in 1935? Whether fighting in Bristol or Gloucester, he tied a doll to his corner post before the first round.

Every character throws up a local memory. In Bobby Kingston's case, it was the pigeon shop in Gloucester Lane, off West Street, Old Market, where he was brought up. He started boxing when he was 12, had 300 fights altogether and was always capable of pulling out the kind of KO punch that made the roof tremble. As for happy-go-lucky Sid Elvins, he once got a surprise verdict over Ginger Britton. But many remember him fondly as the engaging odd-job man "who could repair shoes, cut hair and, when asked, play a passable tune on the piano."

There were boxing shows at Ashton Gate. And, backed by the extrovert flair of Captain Albert Prince-Cox, there were inevitably thrilling bouts at Eastville. "Prince" revolutionised local boxing by the sheer range of his showmanship. It's a chastening fact that he lost most of his money in the end. He'd been a football referee, for six years had been the manager of Bristol Rovers and also ran a circus. As a boxing promoter he had the acumen and enterprise to bring relatively big names to the Colston Hall.

West Country boxers and their managers called him "The Guvnor". He could cut a hard bargain but would also be generous to a defeated contestant — with an extra fiver in the breast pocket as he left the hall. Soon after Prince was appointed manager of Rovers, he put on an evening with eight bouts at Eastville. Len Harvey was top of the bill against Jerry Daley, the "Champion of Wales". Len won in the third round, was paid in one pound notes and took the train out of Temple Meads, unmarked. Life wasn't as kind for poor Daley — he was killed in an accident when working as a labourer at Box Tunnel.

This is not a book about the West's post-war fighters: of the talented Gordon Hazell, son of Billy, an all-in wrestler, who challenged for the British middleweight championship; of the Ratcliffe brothers, especially Terry who won five titles in less than 12 months as an ABA welterweight before turning pro and becoming western area champion; of the ex-Marine Gary Chippendale, the late Johnny Plenty, Stan Cullis, Nick Wiltshire and the others. Nor one to dwell on the brave attempts at promotion by Len Munden and Alf Baker and to a lesser extent Bert Nutt, Len Bryer, Tex Woodward and his nephew Jeff.

The brief I set myself was to capture the mood and flavour of an era. I wanted it to be a tribute to all those who put on the gloves in the Twenties and Thirties. As such it's a record of sweaty endeavour, gruff good-hearted humour and courage. I have gone to the boxers and *used their own words*. To those, often equally courageous, whose names I have inadvertently left out, I apologise.

DAVID FOOT

Chaffey Hayman takes on 'Pudding' Baker, the 'Fighting Barber' in 1887.

Jack Phelps' father, also Jack, (*right*) was no stranger to bareknuckle contests. He used to confide that he never suffered a black eye. His opponent here is Jim Pavey.

A benefit was held at the Empire in 1910 for Bristol's Harry Mansfield. The management committee gather for a photograph. They are: back row – Tommy Davies (*treas*), Joe Bicker (*timekeeper*), A. N. Other, J. Bicker, jnr., Ted Jenkins, A. Heal, W. Bramley (*chairman*), Billy Jones (*trustee*), Jim Lynes. Front – T. Davis, Jack Rawson, George Peters, Jim Richards, George Davis, Albert Church (*trustee*), C. Portch.

15

The local pundits watch intently as two schoolboy members of Barton Hill Boxing Club seek potential fame. There may be a hat in the ring – but no one throws in a towel.

One of Jack Phelps' improvised rings – in an old boot factory at Kingswood. The two welterweights in action are Billy Williams (facing camera) and Jack Holbrook.

16

St Jude's was renowned for its well-equipped boxing club. This is a typical all-action training session, with a line of boys eagerly waiting their turn. The Club was situated at the back of The Crown.

The year is 1922 – and there are as many trophies as earnest young boxers at the popular Barton Hill Boxing Club. Many of Bristol's busy pros of the Thirties can be recognised in this group.

Between the wars the local small-time promoters staged shows in any available venue – like this large shed at the rear of The Red Cow, Bedminster. (There was another in nearby North Street).

The two youthful contestants are Tosh Parker and Tommy Bartlett. Between them is the unmistakably happy face of Dixie Brown. Others in the group include Dick Drew, Bert Budd and Eddie Norton. This boxing match was at the Shepherd's Hall, Old Market.

They called me Len Murder

Len Munden was one of Bristol's great fighters — in and out of the ring. When the war came in 1939 he was the Western area light-heavyweight champion and rated 5th in Britain. He lost his left arm while in the RAF and his promising career as a boxer was over. But he refused to give up. Len became a promoter and put on 30 shows over six years. The TV companies showed scant interest and he lost £10,000. As a trainer-manager he built up an impressive stable of local fighters, including Stan Cullis, Gary Chippendale and Johnny Plenty. He also became a successful coach proprietor and achieved national fame and admiration when, after rebuffs and technical objections extending over six frustrating years, he was awarded his Public Service Vehicle licence as the country's only one-armed coach driver. Len was born at Midsomer Norton and came to Bristol when he was six. His family were farmers with three butchers' shops. He, too, was to be a master butcher. "I was a bit late coming into boxing. I was KO'd three times in my early days when I didn't really know anything. It took me five years to learn the ropes."

On the day I volunteered for the RAF I said I'd never box while the war was on. Yet I found myself, oh lumme days, climbing into the ring at 48 hours' notice as a late substitute to take on, of all people, Bruce Woodcock. And you'll remember he was soon to be the heavyweight champion of the country. I was just 12 stone 6 lbs and hadn't been in the ring for nearly three years! There wasn't really disgrace in being beaten in the second round, was there? At least I was still gamely on my feet. I'd already decided on principle to give my £25 purse to the Bristol General Hospital.

Top of the bill in that open-air show at the White City was a light-heavyweight title fight between Len Harvey and Freddie Mills. I used to be Len Harvey's sparring partner and had a tremendous liking for him. He invited me up to Jack Straw's Castle in Hampstead, where he used to train. And he gave me a lovely reference afterwards. What a gentleman he was — and his American wife was a charming person. It was Len Harvey who really educated me in the ways of boxing. I developed a very good left hook from him — and the solar punch with which I knocked Bournemouth's Bill Fuller cold. I used to stay with the Harveys... a lovely couple.

My brother started me training when I was eleven, you know. The

19

family used to take me one day a week to meet blacksmith Joe Price, of Gloucester. He was known as the strongest man in the world — 58 inches round the chest. And he showed me how to build up my muscles. D'you realise that I could soon break six-inch nails with my bare hands. Could do it in a minute and a quarter. I used to go round the church halls, doing it for charity.

Bob Wade became my right hand man and adviser. He'd been an ex-Navy champ and had fought all over the world. Bob was by then 50, an insurance agent living in Whitehall. You could never hit him — he weaved so cleverly. He taught me all my early boxing and was a big influence. Bob became a referee of course.

I had just a couple of fights, at Frome and Yeovil. Then I was ready to become a pro. Remember there were 3,000 licensed boxers in those days. Just think of that. My first bout was at Bedminster Arcade, against Billy Davis. Billy was considered a bit of a local tearaway. I knocked him out in three rounds and I got the impression that all the bobbies in Bedminster were on my side!

We used to have just a token inspection from a doctor before we went into the ring. If you were warm, you were on. . . . In all I had 93 contests and lost 14. I fought as a 175-lb cruiserweight, later known as light heavyweight, of course.

I can tell you I always looked after myself — and still do. I'm now in my mid-seventies and continue to get up at half past four or a quarter to five in the morning, you know. A few physical jerks in the bedroom to start the day. Ah yes, I've always been fit. Here, I could once lift an Austin 7 with a 12-stone bloke sitting on the bonnet.

I can't begin to tell you how much I liked boxing. So many lovely memories... the Beer Cask in Pennywell Road with its delightful little ring about 12 feet square, it seemed to me. Charlie Hobbs, the landlord, had such a big following for boxing in those days. The Beer Cask used to be known as Bob Wade's boxing academy. But I did a lot of my training below the Hardings' butcher's shop in Cathay, Redcliffe.

I must tell you about the evening Reg Hobbs, Charlie's son, came round to where I was training. He had a strapping young chap with him, a county rugby player called Jack Haskins. I must say I'd never heard of him at the time. 'Len,' said Reg, 'Jack here says he'd like to go a few rounds with you. He's bit useful. What do you say?' It was all right with me, I said. I'd often bang away for 10 . . . 15 . . . 20 rounds in an evening session. A few more with this big rugby fellow wouldn't make too much difference.

By the second round he was dropping his arms to his side and saying: 'That'll do, Len.' I'd let a few go and this Jack Haskins, who I discovered was to feature on some of Prince-Cox's shows, had had

Len Munden in action.

enough. I stepped back and pulled off my big pillow gloves, twice as heavy as those we used for scheduled fights. We exchanged grins. And then Reg Hobbs whispered to me: 'You've cost Jack a quid, Len.' It turned out that this rugby star was so confident of his ability he'd bet Reg £1 that he'd stay three rounds with me . . .

I remember so many useful boxers around the area then. There was Reggie Hall, the flyweight champion of the West. And Ginger Britton, who to my mind was one of the best lightweights ever to put the gloves on in Bristol. Ginger had a serious accident and sadly never boxed again. But, goodness gracious, what hard times they were, too. There were the boxers who'd come across from South Wales on the train. Straight off the shift. Six rounders for just a few bob. And coal dust still on the back of their legs.

I used to fight a lot in the fairgrounds, you know. For charity, though, never for money. I won't forget one week at Horfield, near the barracks. I went out in front every night — and, honestly, I couldn't get a single fight. Not one — and with all those soldiers around! It must have been my reputation that put them off. And probably my right hand...

For two years I was the idol of the city. I was in terrific form in 1937. That was when I won the Western area light heavyweight title bout against Fred Stabbins, the Taunton policeman. Five years before, he'd knocked me out at Weston. I also did very well that year against George Hartley, the northern area champ. I had him down three times in the first round and the ref stopped the fight. That's when they started dubbing me Len Murder and not Munden!

And it was also in 1937 that I took on Ted Broadribb's new heavyweight protegé Dom Lydon. I won't forget that one in a hurry, either. I was giving away a stone but I came straight out in the first round and whacked him with my right. He went down on his right leg and there's a count of nine. He's up again. But the ref gets between us and gives Dom a warning for holding. It was so frustrating for me. They knew and I knew that I could have whacked him once more and he'd have gone down for good.

That's how it was in those days. I realised I had no chance of getting this decision unless I knocked my man out. And there was the ref in the way. Dom was Ted's bright new hope and they'd only come on the understanding that they had an easy one. It was no good objecting. Dom had had five or six fights in London, I imagined, and now he was going out into the provinces for a few more. Ted Broadribb was in his corner. Looking back, what chance did I have?

There were 5,000 fans in the Colston Hall that night. It was the days before the fire there, when there were three balconies. The crowd were

Reggie Hall, flyweight champion of the West, was a courageous boxer. He lost only six of his 84 contests and was never KO'd. Had a good straight left but he scaled only 7 stone 4 lbs and too often had to give weight. As a promising schoolboy boxer he used to wear a swimming costume because he was 'self-conscious about being slightly pigeon-chested'.

Harry 'Ginger' Britton – 'one of the best lightweights to put on the gloves in Bristol'. He had a pallid complexion and a quiet personality. But he was a particularly good timer and had a deceptive way of delivering his powerful left. Once fought a draw with stylish Fred Gaydon at Bristol Zoo. Went to London to work and sparred with Harry Mizler, British lightweight title holder.

stamping their feet in disapproval. It was bedlam. Must have been five minutes or more before the next contest could be started. I'd gone six rounds with Lydon but didn't get the verdict. The crowd knew well enough I should have been allowed to make sure in the opening round.

As the anger continued, Prince-Cox climbed into the ring. He tried to placate my supporters by announcing that Lydon and myself would have a return. We never did, of course! Apparently Ted Broadribb was impressed with my performance and he did subsequently act as my agent for some of my fights away from the West Country. But, lumme days, Dom was lucky that night in Bristol.

I took on Darkie Ellis three times, you know. He beat me on points each time. He was brilliant. The nearest I got to winning was when we topped the bill at Paignton. But he closed my eye in the 7th and I couldn't see a damned thing after that.

My brother Jack managed me for seven years altogether. You know, I've always been a great family man. And dear old Dixie Brown used to be my masseur. He was blind by then.

I must tell you about the occasion I went over to Dublin to fight Joe 'Elbows' Quigley, the light heavyweight champion of Ireland. I got a points decision and picked up my best purse ever — £137. Including expenses, of course. It was very much an exception for an Englishman to win in Ireland. That was also one of the very rare times when I had to stay overnight. We stayed in a hotel full of old ladies and Catholic priests. Fascinating it was. But I was a teetotaller and liked to get home to Betty, my wonderful wife. She'd put hot towels on my face to ease the swelling. I preferred her company, a hot bath and a pint of hot milk to the high life. Oh dear, but for the war I'm sure I'd have been light heavyweight champion of Britain.

In the RAF I became a sergeant parachute instructor. I made more than 90 jumps, 15 of them operational. We were engaged on high-security SAS-style work over occupied territory. We trained top-brass and specialist Allies so that they could parachute back towards their resistance movements.

My luck eventually ran out. Our Hudson crashed over the Middle East and I lost my left arm. No more jumps. No more rounds at the Colston Hall. Life was bleak and depressing for me. But I snapped out of it. I still had my immense strength, which came in useful as I built my own garage. I had a loving family around me. I had my sense of humour . . . and my memories. Now in my mid 70s, I assure you Len Munden is still a fighter.

Len, in the driving cab - one armed and still a fighter.

24

The "One-Round" Soldier

Theo "Soldier" Bradbury was born at Barrow-in-Furness where his father was general manager of a paper mill. The family moved west to Creech St. Michael, near Taunton. Young Theo went to the village school and sang in the church choir. The family then came to Bristol to run a sweet and confectionery shop in Stapleton Road. Theo learned his early boxing in the army; in all he spent 18 years in the Services and rose to the rank of sergeant major (in the military police) — "although I got stripped to sergeant because I went absent for a few days!" His all-action approach in the ring always went down well with the crowds; so did the rather fearsome looking tattoos, all seven of them, on his chest, arms and thighs. "Soldier" was a rugged little fighter, renowned for his stamina. As a rugby forward, he also played for both Exeter and the Army. ("And I got more knocks in the scrum than ever I did in the ring"). His brother was a successful all-in wrestler. After giving up boxing, "Soldier" was a familiar figure driving the No. 18 bus from the Centre to Clifton and the Zoo, or the No. 5 to Filton. Gentle-natured, quiet-voiced, he also became a skilful chess player and picked up a number of local awards. "It kept me mentally alert." He lived in the same house in Patchway for more than half a century and celebrated his golden wedding. When his wife died, he was left with his faithful terrier, Butch.

As a boxer I suppose I tried to model myself on Freddie Mills — you know, take one and give two. They used to say I was a lightweight with the punch of a middleweight. But it's a fact I never hated my opponent. I always showed concern for him when he was down — and I must say, with due modesty, that was fairly often. Boxing to me is a SPORT. A rough one, it's true, but if you're not prepared to take a few knocks, then leave well alone.

I reckon I had more than 80 pro fights and don't think I lost more than four. In my first 17 contests, no-one took me over three rounds. It was apt to finish very early and they used to bill me 'ONE-ROUND BRADBURY' for a time after I put away Staple Hill's Johnny Morgan in the first. I used to fight at the Colston Hall for a tenner but only went to London a few times.

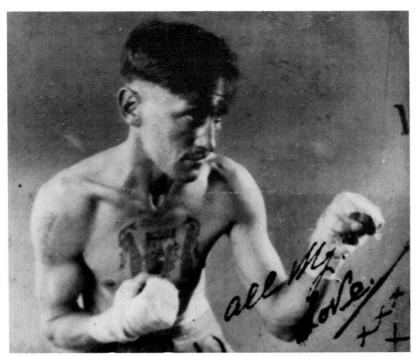

Chess-playing 'Soldier' Bradbury was always good value in the ring. His tattoos were part of his appeal. It cost him £35 to buy himself out of the army, and another £55 for his fare home to this country.

I'd fit in a lot of bouts. For a time, after coming out of the army, I was driving a wagon for some furniture removers and humping coal as well, for £2.15s a week, daylight to dark. And after a full day's work, I'd tear off on the bus or the train to somewhere like Bridgwater or Weston-super-Mare for a contest. I remember weeks when I was fighting on Monday, Wednesday and Friday, say at the Colston Hall, Bridgwater and Taunton.

Only once did I have a go in the booths. That was enough for me. I was up at Horfield Common one Saturday night. Couple of boys up there on the stand — gloves, bandages, boots, Christ knows what! 'Who'll take on this boy?' someone was shouting. 'I will,' I said, on the spur of the moment. They told me I'd get five bob for every round I stayed on my feet. What happened? The fighter on the booth packed it in during the second round. I ended with 15 bob... and an escort from the ground. There were a few threats and it all got a bit nasty. It was made clear to me that I shouldn't have won. The booth people didn't like their lads beaten.

I'd gone into the army in 1929 and became lightweight champion of the Gloucestershire Regiment. I took to boxing like a duck to water. Yet it was against my nature. I'm not an aggressive sort of bloke. In the ring it was all-action stuff, two fists going. And I could box either left- or right-handed. I used to do it in training — it really made no difference. But it didn't half confuse your opponent, I can tell you. I did it once at the Colston Hall. This feller was getting the best of it in the early rounds. So I came out next round a southpaw. He walked right into it. During my army days in India I was matched against Tarley the Filipino. And I stopped him in the 14th which, knowing his reputation, wasn't bad at all. I was really an amateur then, of course, but got a few quid for that one.

'Soldier' Bradbury at the door of his Patchway home, with his faithful companion.

In all I reckon I had about 130 contests and hardly got marked. No, hold on, once I really thought I was going to get a cauliflower ear. But a chap came along and bathed it in hot milk. It seemed to work. And, oh yes, there was the time at Weston when I finished with my eye hanging out on my cheekbone. I knew I was in trouble at the end of the 3rd. So I came out for the start of the 4th, determined to get on with it. Bang, bang. All over. They put my eye back in position and stuck a bandage over it for the time being. Somehow or other, it stuck there. Don't ask me how! A doctor had a look later on and said everything seemed OK. I even started training again next day. I suppose we were pretty tough in those days.

I always looked after myself. A five-mile run first thing in the morning before work. Twice round the Downs and back to Brigstocke Road.

There was real camaraderie then. Tommy Hayes used to live next door to me for years. He was a good, gangling boxer but I'd get inside his lead and give him one in the Derby Kelly (belly). We had plenty of laughs about that later.

Laughs while we were fighting, too. When we were on the bill at the Colston Hall, some of the lads would go across to the Artichoke for a drink before their bout. I remember having a couple of pints and hearing some of the onlookers saying: 'Don't have too many, Soldier.' Then when I was being massaged later, the second would say: 'You stupid bugger — it's running out of your ears.' In fact, I never had too much. A couple of shadow rounds back in the dressing room and I'd worked it off. Then I'd go out and win.

I only fought three or four times after the war. I won the last one, at the Weston Winter Gardens. I could have gone on for years but my wife wanted me to give up. She always waited up for me. I admit I miss it. I'd like it all over again, not half!

He walked to London — to fight

Albert (Boy) Bessell, born in 1917, was brought up in Philadelphia Street, St. Paul's, the area renowned for close-knit family life and good-natured young pugilists. Dixie Brown lived in the same street. Albert was fighting in the booths from the age of eleven — in St. George's Park, Ashton Park and Horfield Common. They used to bill him as "the schoolboy champion of the West of England". As an adult, his style pleased the crowds. "I was a fair boxer and a fair fighter — I could mix it if necessary." He was proud of the fact that after early years of hardship and unemployment, he always worked. Many will remember him for his fruit-and-veg barrow, first in Old Market and later near the London Inn, Bedminster. There are many affectionate stories about "Boy" Bessell. One, which he recalls himself, was of the time when he was called on to substitute at the old Gem. "I fought in my socks and was slipping all over the place. Afterwards my friends and a few journalist friends had a whip-round and presented me with my own pair of boots."

Yes, you're right—I was the bloke who walked to London in search of adventure and a few fights. It's what everyone seems to remember about me!

There were four of us... Gandy Kiswick, Jackie Parker, Sammy Ward and me. It was 1935 and I was 18. All of us out of work and looking for a change of luck. I should say I was the only one who could use his fists. We started out on a Saturday morning. But we soon found that no-one was in the mood to give us a damn lift. So we split up. I stuck with Gandy. Never seen the other two till years later.

It took Gandy and me three days. Slept one night in a hedgerow and under a haystack. Then in a Salvation Army hostel. I had me boxing kit with me, stuffed in a battered little case. I held on to it like grim death. I made for the Dockland Settlement in London and by then, lost in a strange city, I was wondering what the hell I'd let meself in for. But they gave us a cup of tea, a couple of cakes and a ticket to stay at the Salvation Army.

I tramped back to the Settlement next day and they made me out a letter to see Ted Broadribb, who was then a really big name, of course.

TOMMY FARR

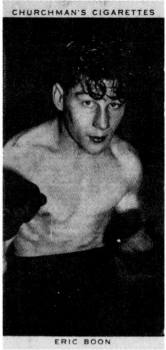

ERIC BOON

I saw various people including Jack King, the matchmaker and manager and promoter Jeff Dixon. They took a look at me and me little bundle of boxing kit and decided to take a chance with me. They got me a room to stay off Covent Garden. And soon I was boxing every Sunday.

Mostly it was at the Devonshire Club or what they called The Ring, or one or two other places like the open-air Mile End Arena or perhaps Hammersmith Stadium. A £1 note for six rounds — and they stopped half a crown of that. The Devonshire Club had a small ring. Suited a fighter, not a boxer who liked a bit of space. I lost to Eric Boon there — and beat Norman Rees, whose brother was the lightweight champion of Wales. I did pretty well in London. Fought on the same bill as Tommy Farr at the Albert Hall three times, you know. Lot of good 'uns around at that time. I did some work as a welder so weren't dependent on me boxing.

At The Ring in Blackfriars you'd knock up £25 for topping the bill. I was just beginning to do this when the war came. Rated No. 3 in the Southern Area Bantamweight class, so like a lot of fighters I probably missed out badly in 1939. Most of my bouts had been in London but I

In this fight at Blackpool, Bessell beat P. Ellis in the 7th round.

did come back to Bristol from time to time. In 1938, I knocked out
Frankie McAvoy at the Colston Hall. That was a bloody good fight.
Lot of money changed hands on that one. Two Bristol boys, see.
Frank's parents had a cockle shop in Pennywell Road.

But let's get back to the booth days when I were a nipper, only
eleven or twelve. Five bob if you was lucky and a share of the
nobbins. And it made you feel like a millionaire. Nothing to stop kids
like me going on the booths. Reckon I had dozens of them booth
fights. Never really got hurt — it wouldn't do for the promoter if any
of the fighters got injured, especially his boys. Most of the scraps
was arranged. Don't think I often saw a straight fight! There'd
be a number of shows a night. So a nice little share-out for six of
us. . . .

You can imagine how welcome that was when I tell you how we
lived in Philadelphia Street. Thirty in one house, I'm telling you. A
number of families. Mother and father and six of us kids... two
double beds in our room... five or six in a bed, head to toe. Mother
did the washing and the cooking on a hob in that room. Then down
three flights of stairs for a drop of water or to go to the lavatory. I went
down with pleurisy at one time. Just couldn't cope at home so they got
me into hospital.

What a way to live! But we was happy. All the families living in the same cramped house got on well together. We trusted one another. Never locked the door. That little corner of Bristol had a bloody wonderful community spirit. You won't find anything like it nowadays.

I were small so learned to fight to protect myself. Always in scraps, couldn't help meself. Dixie Brown actually got to know about me because of the street fights I was getting into. I was never a coward. I'd take on the bullies — and there was plenty of them about.

Apart from the booths, I started boxing professionally when I was 14 and gave up when I was 33. I got one or two bad cut eyes and that affected my sight a bit. Also cracked me jaw. The trouble was that I was wearing a home-made gum shield — we used to make our own then. I was hit on the chin and the shield was loose, like.

There's no doubt about it, whatever anyone says. Boxing is bloody dangerous. You're aiming at the head for God's sake. I remember one boxer, a good-looking kid who reminded me of my brother Bob. When I saw this bloke again only two or three years later, I could hardly recognise him. Cauliflower ears. Flat nose. Glazed eyes. You wouldn't believe it. But you won't get no self-pity from me or the

Albert 'Boy' Bessell and wife Doris in a living room full of boxing mementos.

32

other boxers. We chose to do it. And we enjoyed it.

I didn't do much boxing during the war. I was in the Royal Berks and at one time fractured a kneecap in a motor cycle accident when with the military police traffic control. But I did have one fight at Oxford Town Hall, I remember, I gave away two stone and was top of the bill. Got a draw out of it. And how will I forget what happened at St. James's Hall, Newcastle? I got taken there by five publicans and someone whispered to me: 'Think you ought to lie down for this one, Albert. Be worth your while.'

They was really telling me to take a dive, I suppose. I didn't have any truck with that. I knocked this feller out in the first round! It was Pat Jones of Belfast.

After the war I was wandering round to the booths one day (not working them any more) when I bumped into George Perks. 'What you doing these days, Boy?' I gave him a look. 'Not boxing.' George grinned and said: 'Well, you should be. There's plenty of money in the game.' And I took his advice. That's how I went back to it.

As South West area featherweight champion, at the Winter Gardens, Weston-super-Mare, I caused Irishman Morty Kelleher, six times ABA champ, to retire at the end of the 5th round. It was top of the bill at the first night of the Weston Sportsmen's Club. I cut both his eyes. We both got a helluva lot of applause at the end. Morty was a good-looking boy.

The crowd could also be a bit one-sided at Weston. I outpointed their local boy Sammy Reynolds over eight rounds. It was a great fight and I reckon I was well on top at the end. Some of 'em didn't agree and they started booing. Completely unjustified, but you've got to take that in your stride.

I was tough as old boots. At the Pavilion, Bath in 1948 I fought eight rounds, as holder of No. 2 area (Southern) area featherweight title, with Danny Nagle, of Ireland. Nagle won on points. But I'd been injured in the previous fight and the Boxing Board wanted me to call off. I wouldn't hear of it — I turned up with a doctor's certificate and said: 'I'm OK — just let me get in that ring.' Of course, I shouldn't have fought but I probably needed the money. And, in any case, it was Mr. L. A. Phillips' first promotion and I didn't want to let him down.

I suppose the hardest fight I ever had was in 1947 at Cheltenham Town Hall. My opponent? An up-and-coming Jackie Turpin. He was ambitious, full of fire. I was on the way out, so some were saying. But they got it all wrong. I had a coach load up from Bristol and didn't lack support. And I beat young Jackie. The commentator on the radio, Raymond Glendenning, said he'd never seen a scrap like it.

33

And here's a final memory, though you probably won't believe it. I once had two fights on a Sunday afternoon. Could have been pretty embarrassing, I'm telling you. Ted Broadribb had set up one contest for me and promoter Jack King another, at a different venue. They'd got completely mixed up, not knowing what the other was doing. Somehow or other it worked out OK. I knocked my opponent out at The Ring and then got the fight stopped in the 3rd, in my favour, at Hammersmith. Don't ask me what would have happened if I'd got a cut eye or something in the first bout. And you want to know what I earned for that chase-around? Seventeen-and-six . . . just seventeen-and-six. They used to stop half-a-crown for a second's money in those days. I was driven at speed from one place to the next. Not a whisper of what had happened in the public announcement. We all had our fingers crossed, hoping that I'd come through all right. It got into the papers next day!

Twenty quid in me boots

Pat Patterson, a Bristol-born bantamweight, was particularly proud of the fact that he never took the count in well over 100 professional fights. His interest in boxing started when he used to go along under Albert Jennings' supervision to the old Dockland Settlement in Lewin's Mead, next door to the church. His memory, when the Settlement moved to Rosemary Street, was of "the halfpenny dinners and being served by Royalty" — at least the Duke and Duchess of Beaufort. "They used to bring in rabbits and chicken off the estate." Pat was a well-known newspaper seller, of the *Evening Times and Echo*, and the *Bristol Evening News*, at the bottom of Union Street ("I got a penny for every three sold"). He went into the Royal Navy and was one of the few survivors picked up when HMS *Coventry* was sunk, having dived over the side. He ended up a docker at Avonmouth.

C After boxing as an amateur at the Settlement, I was taken up by Eddie Norton who with Albert Rowlands ran the Arcade at Bedminster. Eddie got me a fight in an old garage just behind the Full Moon, in Moon Street, Stokes Croft. Dixie Brown used to stage the bouts with a bloke called Harper. People paid a shilling to come in, three-and-six for the ringside. Eddie put me in against Kid Alexander, another local boy. I got 7s.6d for that one. Didn't have a licence, just useful cash in the hand. But I was really a pro from then on.

Then I got a few scraps at the Arcade — against Inch Jones, Freddie Tite, Fred Gaydon and so on. I remember having 10 two-minute rounds with Tosh Parker and got 50 bob for that. Still unlicensed, until Jimmy Wilde came along one evening and told us we'd have to join the Boxing Board of Control. 'You boys have got to get a licence — you can't keep going on like this,' Jimmy said. So I paid me five bob and saw meself as a real pro. In the first fight I was well down the bill but got a fiver for it. A Plymouth kiddie called Bill Hood was top. Tudor Reardon was his real name. Lot of 'em fought under different names. I always kept me own.

My hardest? Had to be the one against Boyo Rees at the Arcade. Jimmy Wilde was the ref and Bert Harding was in me corner. Drew

Pat Patterson in his Royal Navy days (*left*) and, today near his Bristol home.

the first time and beat me the second. Loved it at the Bedminster shows. Lot of noise, lot of atmosphere.

Perhaps they weren't quite so hot on medical matters then. But there was some good refs around. Didn't stand any bloody nonsense. If someone went down and weren't too badly hurt, the ref would say: 'Hey, up you get ... Up!' Very strict. Albert Jennings was a helluva good man — straight as a die. Did some fighters take a dive? Maybe occasionally. Not me. Might have went on just now and then. Some boxers needed the money and went into the ring when they weren't completely fit. Bags of guts. Didn't worry about the consequences.

I had a straight left and a good right hook. Once at Swindon I was on the same bill as Len Harvey. My fight was with Fred Gaydon. And I boxed a lot in the Navy. King Farouk was at the ringside for one of my contests in Alexandria. And I remember fighting a three-round exhibition bout with Johnny King, the European champion, at the Muller Road Orphanage during the war. The place was used as a naval recruitment centre at the time.

Not likely to forget me last fight. No bloody fear. I was just back from five and a half years in the Navy. I was a bit short of money and went along to the Colston Hall to see a show. There was always the chance of stepping in for someone at the last minute. 'Seaman'

Pat (*extreme left*) joins other West Country boxers in a happy reunion. *Left to right*: Patterson, Fred 'Boy' Cox, Bert Harding, Albert Bessell, Arnold Rose, Terry Harding (*at rear*), 'Tiger' Pomphrey, Sid Elvins, George Rose, Ivor Gaydon (*partly hidden*), Inch Jones, Reggie Hall and Joe Cottle (*front centre*).

Froggatt from Portsmouth was supposed to be boxing but didn't turn up. George Rose was topping the bill and he said: 'How about you taking on one of these blokes here?' I didn't have much change in me pocket. 'Don't mind, George.'

But when the name of me opponent was announced from the ring, I nearly fell through the bloody canvas. Danahar! Still don't know to this day whether it was the famous Arthur or a brother . . . I got beaten in the 4th. Badly cut eye — and the ref stopped the fight. Needed two operations and I've now lost the sight from it.

Prince-Cox, the promoter, slipped 20 quid into me boxing boots afterwards. Then as I was coming out of the Colston Hall, some bloke come up to me: 'While you've been away, Pat, we've kept your licence payments up. You owe us £7.' Just think of that. I'd just bashed away for four rounds with a feller called Danahar and got me eye permanently damaged. All for 20 quid — and here I was parting bloody company with seven straightaway.

Although I say it meself, I could be quite stylish, like. Jack Phelps used to say I sometimes looked like a million dollars. A good bloke, Jack, for giving you a lift!

Tosh had three fights in a day

Tom "Tosh" Parker, all 5 ft 2½ ins of him ("I had a longer reach than people thought") had 183 fights as a pro — and he can remember losing only five or six of them. His parents came from Bristol but moved to South Wales, where his father worked as a butcher and then in the mines. Tosh lived with his grandmother in Barton Hill until he was six. He left school at 14 to go down the mines. "I weighed 4 stone 4 lbs then and when I was 17, my father put me on his old-fashioned butcher's scales and I weighed 5 stone 7½ lbs. He loved boxing but his mother, a Salvationist, shook her head and said: "Tom, God never gave you a body to be knocked about." His reply was: "But mother, wouldn't you prefer me keeping fit and training hard than going into pubs and maybe getting into bad company?" It was a persuasive argument and Eddie Norton brought Tosh to Bristol to top the bill at the opening of the Bedminster Arcade. Eddie also found him a job — and he stayed. Eventually he was a chargehand at BAC for 20 years.

In the early days I'd work a shift underground from 7am till 2pm, come up and bath, walk across the mountains to Pontypridd and catch the bus to where I was fighting. Life really is much easier for the new generation. You can't expect 'em to be so tough.

I remember turning up for my first fight at the Baden-Powell Club near Porth. I was completely unknown, a little chap matched against the experienced Spike Whale. And I beat him. Afterwards they asked me: 'How many bouts have you had?' I told 'em only a couple. 'Well,' they said, 'this Spike is a former schoolboy champion and has had more than 40 scraps.' I was offered 25 bob win, lose or draw and became a bit of an attraction at the club.

I was learning all the time. Never to hit an opponent if he was going away from me. But get him when he was coming towards me. I used to think all the time of my father's advice: 'Don't let the other chap hit you. Boxing is a science. Make him miss — and then connect yourself. And remember, young Tom, one good punch is worth a dozen taps.'

During the miners' strike in 1926 I had 22 fights over just six

Tosh Parker, the bonny little 'paperweight' (*left*) and debonair Inch Jones with whom he hoped in vain for a return.

months. Three of them on one day. Morning, afternoon and evening. Everyone was unemployed. The doors used to open at 11 o'clock in the morning. The three contests were in different halls — and I stopped all the opponents inside the distance. But Dad told me to slow down. During the strike, the purse went down from 30 bob to a pound.

Eddie Norton, who always called me Boyo, had seen me doing my stuff in Wales and brought me over for his first show at the Arcade. I topped it with young Jim Driscoll from Ferndale. He was taller than me. I got a cut eye and the ref stopped it in the 7th. Pity, that. I could have gone on, I was so strong. They gave me £2.15s for that one. They were always a good, loyal crowd at the Arcade Hall. If they took to you, you were the king. They must have realised my family came from Bristol — my mother from Montague Terrace near the BRI, my father from Rosemary Street.

My trouble was that I was always giving away weight. I was a *paperweight*, as they used to call it. Because I was so small, I seldom had the chance to take on anybody more or less my own weight. 'You're a good boy, Tom,' the famous Welsh referee C. B. Thomas once said, 'but you're simply giving away too much weight.'

I only got knocked out on one occasion — and by someone I didn't really rate as an outstanding boxer. Funny, that. It was Inch Jones who put me on my back. I'd beaten Freddie Gaydon who'd twice KO'd Inch. That's how it goes.

Twelve months later I looked in at the Arcade one training night. 'Come on, Tosh, put the gloves on.' It was Inch Jones. I made a complete fool of him. Blood everywhere. Eddie Norton leaned over the ropes and said to Inch: 'There, I told you this kid would take you six times out of seven.' I wanted a return with Inch Jones but Eddie was against it because of the weight difference.

I remember my second fight at the Arcade, in 1929. It was against Tiger Pomphrey — and I KO'd him in the 1st. And that brings back a memory of what happened in 1932 when I was working on the buildings in Southmead. Suddenly I was asked to come in as a sub, again against Tiger. I hit him from pillar to post and he needed to go to hospital to get rid of some of the bruises. And, do you know, the decision went against me. It was the most disgraceful verdict I've ever known.

'Here,' I said to Bob Wade, the referee, 'I'd like to know what you give points for these days?' I listed what I thought they should be for. Guess what Bob's reply was. 'Well, we've got to give the youngsters a chance.'

'Come off it! Tiger isn't much younger than me. What are you talking about?' Tiger wasn't skilful, just rugged. He might not have had much defence but he had the heart of a lion. Once he told me I was the only fellow who ever hurt him.

Reg Hall was my idea of a good, clean boxer. He was clever, fast, aggressive. A consistent fighter but he suffered because he couldn't punch. I fought him for the flyweight championship of the West of England and got beaten all right. Some said I should have had it. I didn't agree and certainly didn't argue when he got the verdict.

I was cool as a boxer, never nervous. I'd look across the ring at my opponent before the start and work out whether he was on edge. D'you know the best purse I ever got? Just £12 for fighting Eric Beswick over 15 rounds at Stockport.

Medical supervision was a bit slap-happy, of course. A doctor would take a look at you an hour before the contest. If you got a cut on the eye, no-one could care less, it seemed, if the seconds could patch it up between the rounds. There were a few dirty fighters. Thumb in the eye. One in the kidneys, you know. And I could tell you of a few boxers who liked the booze too much and went into the ring under the influence. But we all got on well together.

It was important to retain a sense of humour. I used to say that, because of my size, they couldn't see me once they put the gloves on me. People used to tell me I had a heart bigger than my body and that

Tosh, perky as ever (*centre front*) among this group of boxing friends. Others L to R: Alf and Fred Tite, Ivor George, Mike Gerrish, Bill Bridges and Bert Nutt, who used to organise the popular reunions.

was a nice compliment to hear. George Rose's father, who mended umbrellas and was known as The Umbrella Man, always said he rated me. When I was working on Bath Bridge, putting electric cables over the river in about 1929, a works colleague for a time was Benny McNeill. He thought I'd done well to beat Fred Gaydon and said: 'I've heard a lot about you. Why don't you fight in Paris like I did?' Benny persuaded me to go to Portishead and box a six-round exhibition with him in a little hall there. Afterwards he put his arm over my shoulder and said: 'You never ought to do another day's work. You're a real boxer. You're clever at slipping punches and haven't got a mark on you.' 🥊🥊

41

Footballers both of them –
Tommy Bartlett (*above*) in his
Downs League and Gloucestershire county days, and fellow
boxer Bert Nutt, who had two
seasons with Ipswich Town after
the war.

The K.O. King

Tommy Bartlett was born in Dale Street, St. Paul's and started boxing under Bert Budd at the well-equipped St. Jude's Boxing Club. He had an upright stance and a big punch. Hence his nickname: The Knock-out King. Most of his fighting was done before he was 21, at a time when he was frequently out of work. Tommy kept himself very fit and was still playing football when he was 50. A versatile footballer, at his best as an attacking half-back, he was talented enough to captain Gloucestershire, and made 28 appearances for the county. He was well-known as a robust player for Dockland Settlement and Westbury Old Boys, "but I only got sent off once," he tells you with a grin. He fought as a featherweight and lost only 10 of his 90 contests.

❝❝Got knocked out just once, you know. At the Barton Hill Baths, it was. I was winning this one easy, no trouble. Then I went back against the ropes which were very tight. They shot me straight back — and I walked into it.

I boxed in most of the local halls. The Arcade, the Gem, the Drill Hall, Shepherd's Hall, Old Market. It was at the Drill Hall that I put Arnold Rose away in about 20 seconds. Later at the Colston Hall, I caught Arnold with a left hook followed by a right — again in the first round.

Prince-Cox brought glamour to the fight game in Bristol. I fought on the same bill for him, at the Colston Hall, as Tommy Farr when he beat Venus de Boer. I learned plenty from Tommy. We used the same dressing room and we talked a lot. In the ring he moved from the hips. He showed me it was all about blocking and parrying. I remember Tommy standing with me in the dressing room and looking across at the bloke I was due to take on. He viewed them two big cauliflower ears, gave me a grin and said: 'Who the hell's that, Tommy?'

Once I caused a bit of a local stir by offering to meet George Pomphrey and his brother Albert for six or ten rounds — on the same night. The idea caught on and it was good publicity. I was willing for the Pomphreys to have a £20 sidebet on the fights and said they could choose the ref. But 'Tiger' backed out, apparently because I was too heavy for him. George got KO'd in the fourth. He was up and down like a bloody Weston donkey. And his old man was saying he'd get a good hiding when he got home!

I did take on 'Tiger' in what, looking back, seemed like a shed at Farrington Gurney. A proper scrap, though. I put him out in the sixth. They used to say I had a deadly right hand. The crowds were always waiting for it, waiting for the big one to catch the other bloke on the chin.

As a lad I had a bout at least every fortnight. Fifteen bob for six rounds, thirty bob for ten. They were often bloody hard times. I remember once going along to the Colston Hall in the late Thirties, hoping that someone would cry-off. I told my wife: 'I may be lucky.' And then I came home later that night. 'Nothing doing' — and we just looked at each other. Lads used to take their boots and dressing gowns along, ever hopeful. Some didn't have dressing gowns. They had an old overcoat instead.

I fought Al Harding when he came back from Canada and beat him, at the Drill Hall. George Rose was the best, of course he was. But he didn't have the punch. You should have seen all that bloody lovely

Tommy Bartlett takes it easy at home – his famous fists have earned that rest.

ringcraft. If Prince-Cox wanted to get in touch with me, he'd do it through Bert Budd. Bert's wife made me first boxing shorts, you know. Bert had the finest club any young lads could wish for in Bristol. I also used to train at the Crown, Lawford's Gate — me uncle, Bill Parker kept it for years.

Some of them promoters liked you to make it last. Once at Yeovil I was taken down by a detective — I liked to keep in with the police! George Perks, the barber, was MC. And as I laid into the other feller, the chap who was running the show was shouting to me: 'Hey, hold on, don't put him out too quick.' I weren't having none of that. This promoter wanted me to kiss and dab him a bit and keep the thing going. I caught my opponent with a left hook and then a right. He went straight out of the ring.

I mentioned just now how we used to hope one of the boxers wouldn't turn up and we could take his place — and some of his money. This did happen to me at the Colston Hall one time. They put me into the ring against Pat Patterson. And we was old mates, brought up together around the back streets of St. Paul's. They made it a draw — and I daresay they fiddled the result a bit....

During the war I was a sergeant in the 2nd Battalion of the West Yorks. In the El Alamein campaign, twelve or so of us got cornered and taken prisoner. We'd been made to throw down our rifles and things didn't look too hot for us. But at the right moment I lashed out with me feet — perhaps I really was a better footballer than boxer, after all — and the German went down. We made it at a helluva speed the 150 yards back to our lines. I suppose you could say that was a verdict which could have gone the other way.

45

When fights were bizarre!

Arnold Rose was born at Pontypridd in 1912 and had five brothers. There were strong Weston-super-Mare links on his mother's side. His grandmother had a cottage at Sand Bay and he used to come over from South Wales to stay with her in the summer. He left school at 14 to help on a butcher's stall in the market. He came to live in the West Country in the late Twenties and from 1932 became a busy and well-known boxer in various venues around the region. At one time he was a leading contender for the area lightweight title. Arnold was forced to give up boxing because of an eye injury. But his interest in the sport was fully maintained — he was a whip, second and referee for 13 years, up to 1965. He was the Western Area's only licensed referee for some time, carrying on the traditions of personalities like Bob Wade, Sam Morgan, Ernie Wallace and Albert Jennings. In the war he served with the North Somerset Yeomanry, boxed for his regiment and became a middleweight champion in the Services while still only a lightweight. Later he qualified as a physiotherapist and had a practice at Milton, Weston-super-Mare, where for a time he also acted as trainer and sponge-man for the local rugby club, as well as assisting football, swimming and water polo teams, and even tending the aches and pains of the Bristol Bulldogs speedway riders. Arnold was good at English and Latin at school, though circumstances meant he had to leave at 14. His gentle manner and lyrical way with words often caused the customers at the butcher's shop where he worked to say: "We just won't believe you're a boxer."

Do you know the most bizarre contest I ever had? It was the second time I met Tiger Boon, the tearaway southpaw from Yeovil. You won't believe what happened at the Colston Hall that night. I'd beaten him at our first meeting. This time he saw my wife before the fight and said with a smile: 'It's my turn tonight, Mrs. Rose.' And he really believed it was. Jock McAvoy was top of the bill — and Tiger and I didn't get on for our 10-rounder until half-past-eleven! Just think of that.... but the crowd reckoned it was worth waiting for. In retrospect, I'm not so sure it was.

In the first round, Tiger was grinning for some reason. He looked pretty confident. But he was also open. So I pounced like a cat. I

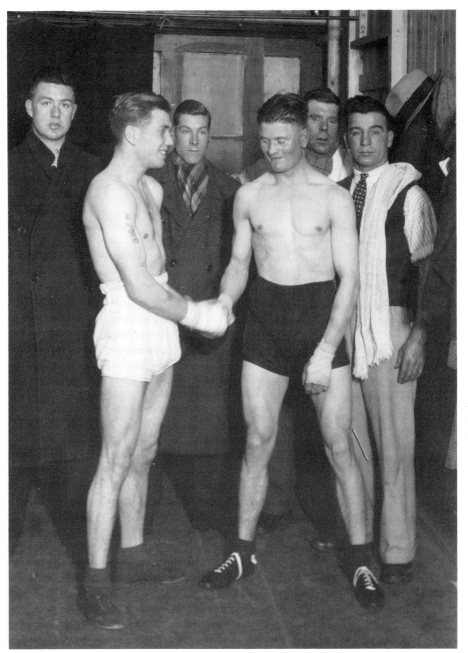

The night at Bridgwater in 1934 when 'Tiger' Boon, the tearaway Yeovil southpaw (*left*) lost to Arnold Rose. In the Rose corner was Weston's Eddie Fear (*with towel*), himself an ex-army champion.

caught him with a beauty and he went out like a light. The bell went at 7 and they got him back to his corner. Back he came for the next round, patched-up. But I wasn't daft — I knew Tiger wouldn't give up easily. So I decided to go for his stomach — he was always a bit weak there. I gave him a pasting and early in the third round, he looked up and lifted his arms. He looked a weary man. 'Had enough, Tiger?' He had a glazed expression and said: 'Yes.' My response was to whisper: 'Bad luck.' Then I tapped him warmly on the shoulder and pointed him back towards his corner. He just didn't go. He shaped up again and I stood there, transfixed, not knowing what to do or say for several seconds. It was all very odd. The crowd didn't know what was happening. But I had to do something — so I sent a piledriver into his lower ribs.

Suddenly Tiger's face went ashen. He sagged lower and lower. And then he hit the deck. To add to the confusion, George Perks the MC jumped into the ring and the ref Rattler Morgan didn't order him out. I put on my dark grey dressing gown and waited for somebody to tell me what was going on. The commotion in the ring lasted for a good two minutes. And then, to my astonishment, I heard someone say: 'It's all right for him to box on.'

It was crazy, unbelievable. I wanted to know what the hell was going on. Why hadn't they counted Tiger out? For some incredible reason I'll never understand, a decision was made to carry on with the fight. In a daze I dutifully put my gloves on again and took off my dressing gown. And here comes the biggest, cruellest irony of all. The fight restarted and I caught Tiger with another beefy punch. He dropped his head down and clearly didn't know what he was doing. Then, involuntarily, he flung his head up again and caught me on the eye. It was a bad cut. And the contest was stopped.... in Tiger's favour.

The Board of Control wasn't so strong in those days and I could have created a fuss. I didn't want to do that. I liked Prince-Cox, the promoter. He was larger than life. That ridiculous bout with Tiger Boon was my only moan with Prince-Cox. Mind you, Tiger rather rubbed it in when later, outside having a cuppa, someone said to him: 'So you beat Arnold, then.' And he replied proudly that he'd cut me up a bit!

There was the earlier time Tiger wasn't able to fight a return with me and Bert Bateman stepped in. Tough-looking bloke was Bert. Shoulders like Max Baer. I told myself 'Better be careful with this one, Arnold.' So I decided to BOX him. In, out and away — I never forgot how to do that.

He wasn't doing anything to me. He was missing a lot. By the end of

Memories of the last pre-war show at the Knightstone Theatre, Weston-super-Mare. This 1935 weigh-in group includes L to R: George Perks ("the little man with the big voice"), Bath boxer Jimmy Gibbons, Sam 'Rattler' Morgan, Arnold Rose and referee Bob Wade. Gibbons lost in the 5th round.

the second, I began to wonder whether he could take my right. So I let one go. I caught him bang on the chin and he went flat on his face. Then the bell went. In those days I used to pick 'em up and help carry them back to their corner. Bit of psychology, really. The crowd liked it. Poor old Bert passed out and fell off his stool into the ring. They got him round eventually and someone was quick to say: 'We'll match you up again at 10 stone.' I replied: 'That's really too heavy for me. But it's OK.' Of course, I still took on Tiger.

To be honest, I always did pretty well against Boon. I could knock him out and was one of the few at the time who could. I'd studied him when he fought Tommy Bartlett on the Pier at Weston. Someone said: 'This bloke will beat any lightweight in this part of the country.' It was meant for my ears. I said: 'Give me three months and I'll crack Tiger.' And I did when I topped the bill with him at Bridgwater. I knew his flaws and went in with a right to the solar plexus. It was all over, in effect. And on the strength of that, George Perks really introduced me to Prince-Cox.

Another Yeovil southpaw, Cyril Downton provided me with perhaps my hardest fight and one with a remarkable finish. We'd met once in Yeovil where I remember George Perks whispering as I climbed into the ring: 'Put one on his bloody chin, Arnold, I want to get home early tonight!' But George had to wait. I hit Cyril again and again. He just wouldn't go down and he only lost on a cut eye.

He was an awkward boy, more or less square-on. I was very orthodox but I always tried to adjust my style a bit when I came up against the southpaws. I'd ignore their right lead. Let them hit me on

Eddie Middle (signature)

Three boxers from Weston: (*far left*) Arnold Rose, Bert Cook - yet another butcher - a middleweight who gravitated to Bath. He fought for the Western area title against Plymouth's Dick Burt - it was a draw and the title remained vacant; and bantamweight Eddie Middle (*this page*) 'who if only he'd closed his fists when he punched might have ended up a champion'.

the head. Then I'd whip one in just under the heart. Once I caught Tiger there and thought I'd killed him.

When it came to that second fight with Downton, over 10 rounds in Bristol, I thought I had it made. I put him down four times in the first round, three times in the second and third. But the fact was that I couldn't do it again. I was flipping exhausted. At the end he caught me with a thundering swing and I'd hit him with an uppercut as he came in. We went down together in the seventh. I was up at three and Cyril at eight. I won on points and he told me later he couldn't remember a bloomin' thing after walking into my very first punch!

51

If that was tough, what do I say about my bout with Bath's Alf Bishop at the Pavilion, Clevedon? He boxed my head off for six rounds. Then he caught me with a straight left and a left hook. I went out for a few seconds but heard the ref count 'seven'. I staggered up and leaned against the ropes. Alf came in to finish me off. I left myself open but took him by surprise with a right swing. He went right back across the ring and against the ropes on the other side and went down for a few seconds. We had a ding-dong after that but he got the verdict.

There were some useful boxers around Weston in those days... Bert Cook, a butcher like me, Eddie Fear, Minto Morris, Fred Stabbins, Eddie Middle, Ginger Harris and Jack Symonds. I got the impression that Jack once resented me being top of the bill at Bridgwater. He said to the promoter: 'Do you want to see Arnold in the ring with a black eye?' And Jack did his best to give me one during a bout in the gym off Locking Road. In the end he grinned and said: 'I've had enough.'

In 1938–39 George Perks and Prince-Cox asked me if I'd like to fight Jack Dale for the lightweight title of the West. Dale had said that I claimed I was the best, weight-for-weight, in the area. That wasn't true — George had said that. But in any case, the war came and there was no title bout.

Looking back, I don't feel I boxed seriously enough, really. In 1936 a syndicate from Bolton had offered to look after me for £6 a week. They said that when I became a championship contender, they'd want 25 per cent of my earnings. I turned it down. I never had a manager. Sometimes I used to think I lived in the wrong place — it would have worked to my advantage if I'd lived in Bristol.

My strength was that I had a good punch and instinctive timing in the same way as featherweight Fred Gaydon and Inch Jones. I could stand still to deliver a knockout. I was KO'd myself four times in just under 60 contests. Once I fought 10 rounds at Bath on a Friday night, was working at 6am in the butcher's shop on Saturday and had another 10 rounds at Taunton in the evening.

I've so many memories, many of them amusing, from my days as a referee. Once at Cheltenham the ring collapsed during the 3rd round of a heavyweight contest. The promoters got it fixed quite quickly. I had the two boxers back into the ring and said: 'Sorry, lads, afraid we've got to start the 3rd all over again.' It wasn't very popular. 'Oh no, ref, have a heart!' they argued, but in vain.

I was reffing at the Colston Hall on a night when the crowd had to put up with a succession of disappointing bouts. Then it came to the last one, Cliff Purnell from Bath against a heavyweight from London.

The lad from London had a bit of a moan to me and said he wouldn't have bothered to come down if he'd known Purnell was a southpaw. That was a good start.

But we got underway — and I have to admit the standard was pretty dreadful. They slugged, they missed. I discreetly let one or two things go because everything was so comic and the spectators were clearly enjoying it. The boxers thumped away at each other — and even thumped me accidentally. Purnell won in six rounds on points and I must say that in terms of entertainment it saved the show for Prince-Cox. Afterwards I went into the dressing room, as was my habit, and one of the boxers grinned and said: 'How the bloody hell did you put up with that?' The likeable Cliff confided to me: 'Do you know, ref, I eat and sleep boxing!' I couldn't help myself: 'And all you need to do, Cliff, is LEARN boxing!'

Twice in my career as a West Country ref, I disqualified both boxers — that doesn't often happen. The first time was at St. Austell where I found myself warning the two welterweights as early as the opening round. I'd had enough by the 3rd and someone quickly assured me I'd done the right thing. Those boxers were just trying to con me. And it also happened at Weymouth in a scheduled 10-rounder. I warned the pair twice and, after making them keep going for eight rounds, I warned them together and abandoned the contest.

I don't know who the heck they thought they were kidding. I could tell when a boxer was trying. Here were two going through the motions. For heaven's sake, I'd done gee-boxing myself on the booths and knew the tricks...

Terry Harding was one of five brothers, well known as butchers and for their love of boxing. The other brothers were Ernie, Alf (or Al), Percy and John. Al was generally acknowledged as the best boxer and fought for a time as a lightweight professional in Canada. But Terry was capable enough to be paired with George Rose at the Colston Hall. The brothers' father was a master butcher and cattle dealer; the Harding boys had their work-outs, like many others, in the gym under the butcher's shop at Cathay, Redcliffe. Percy did some promoting and the family also ran booths at Horfield Common and St. John's Lane, Avonmouth at one time. Nowadays Terry lives at Dundry. He used to ride with both the Quantock and the Berkeley Hunts and retains his interest in horses.

Al made his debut on one of Prince-Cox's bills at the Colston Hall, in aid of Bristol Rovers FC, and that was quite a night. The top-of-the-bill turned into a sensational affair. As far as I can remember, it lasted only about 90 seconds. Harry Crossley, cruiserweight champion of Great Britain and Lonsdale Belt holder, knocked out the Frenchman Emile Egrel, who we understood had never been put on his back before in 200 contests. He'd recently taken Len Harvey the full distance. The Frenchman got quite worked up after his defeat and wanted to climb back into the ring. But he had been caught with a lovely left hook to the side of the jaw and took two minutes to recover.

The crowd, I remember, were pretty disappointed not to see more of a fight. Crossley said he couldn't understand how easy it had been. But then along came our Al to win them back with a typical all-action performance — and a win.

It was an interesting sort of bill. Bedminster's Billy Price, who kept scoring with his left, got a points decision over Flutey Green, who'd come in as a late substitute. Flutey was a black boxer and the reports of the day referred to him as 'the darkie'. Just think of a description like that nowadays! There was 'Young Maggs' who lost to Billy Symes. And 'Young Cottle' fighting a draw with 'Young Pomphrey'. Do you know, the evening also included an exhibition of ju-jitsu and

Brothers Al (*left*) and Terry Harding. One of a number of well known boxing families in those days. Terry, a long established Bristol butcher, was apt to go hunting when his boxing days were over.

catch-as-catch-can wrestling between Harry Rowland and Bristol's Billy Allen.

Personal memories — where do I start? I went down to box at Yeovil on one occasion. My opponent was full of bulging muscles and what looked like confidence. But in the first round I hit him on the mouth. He went right through the ropes and wouldn't come back. It seems he was a bit worried about his appearance!

I must admit I got the impression it wasn't unheard of for a manager to put money on an opponent and a few other odd things went on. Once at the City ground I knocked down an opponent with a legitimate punch in the 6th round. I saw him look at his corner and there was an exchange of winks. Then to my astonishment, the ref stepped in and disqualified me for what was supposed to have been a low blow. He'd already counted to six for heaven's sake. I appealed to the crowd — and for a doctor or someone or other to examine my opponent. I was pretty angry and I followed him out of the ring, challenging him about what had happened. All I heard him say was: 'He hit me too bloody hard.'

Like many of the boxers in my day, I worked to a tight schedule. I'd work in the butcher's shop all day and then motor to somewhere like Hereford in the family car for a fight. I was a 10 stone seven welterweight and thought it a great honour when I got matched with George Rose. I was 20 at the time and he was too clever for me, of course. He tied me up and I lost. The fight was worth nine quid to me. But I was a bit young and learned so much afterwards.

You never forget your first contest. Mine was against a chap called Cole from Tetbury. I won on a knock-out and that was a great moment for me. I once lost by only half a point to Tommy Bartlett. He couldn't half bloody hit, I can tell you. Bill Price was another gutsy boxer. Worked on the buildings and good enough to take on anyone around at the time. Bob Kingston, from Gloucester Lane, was a noted puncher but Bill said he could take him. And he did . . . twice, as far as I recall.

I beat local boy Tommy Luffman at the Arcade on points. A fortnight later I went along to watch. One boxer didn't turn up and Eddie Norton tapped me on the shoulder. 'How about it, Terry — fancy taking on Luffman again?' They hurriedly lent me some shorts and gloves. But in the 2nd I got caught with a beauty and our Alf chucked the towel in. I reckon I was about 17 then and Luffman was probably ten years older. The Arcade Hall was always full of bloody smoke — and noisy. I should say there were 50 regular Bristol boxers around then and plenty of others wanting a chance. I had a very high regard for the flyweight Reggie Hall and put him only behind George Rose and 'Dixie' of the local boys.

The 'Beer Cask' tradition

Reg Hobbs, whose father was Charlie (of Beer Cask fame) boxed as a featherweight himself. He had a fine record as an amateur and was one of three boxers chosen by Fred Dyer — a Welsh man with a fine baritone voice and a sound record as a handler of boxers — to form a small stable in London. Fellow Bristolian George Rose and Midlander Bert Kirby were the others who went. Reg won about threequarters of his fights; he had a good left hand and was a skilful counter-puncher, talented enough to be matched against two Welsh champions. Nowadays he lives in Kingswood where his hobbies include classical music and "the avid reading of books on history".

Dad began as a bootmaker and then ran the Beer Cask for nearly 40 years. He loved boxing and was actually co-promoting Harry Mansfield at a Park Street venue in the early days. That's really going back. I looked on him as a great benefactor for the sport. He filled a void, turning an old shed at the back of the pub into a gym. So many including some champions came there to train — or just to watch. And there was Bob Wade, of course, 'a wonderful teacher en masse'. No-one ever paid anything for lights or anything like that. Dad was just happy to keep boxing going.

I suppose I fought ten times or so at the Drill Hall, Old Market. As an amateur I'd often been paired with George Rose and then, as a pro, I beat him. I drew with him after that. Some at the ringside thought I'd beaten Rose again but not Kid Lewis the ref. George, Bert Kirby — who was to become flyweight champion of Britain — and I lodged together in London, when Fred Dyer took us in charge. He was a bit of a fanatic about diet, I remember. Insisted on special food for us.

I used to train at the old National Sporting Club, a remarkable institution. It had a very Bohemian atmosphere. Big money was always changing hands during the fights there. I met and talked to many of the most brilliant boxers of the day during that period. Four times I fought at The Ring, Blackfriars — also the popular Premierland and Lime Grove Baths, Shepherds Bush. At Hackney, the ring was so small that the spectators were right up against the

Reg Hobbs - it's classical music and a good history book for him nowadays.

ropes. I got hit very low there by Billy Mack, fighting on his home ground. He should have been disqualified, of course. But instead, the referee decided to give me a minute's rest. What do you think of that?

The most vivid memories for me are of the early days at the unlicensed shows. I once topped the bill at Yeovil and got 30 bob for it. An army champion's opponent didn't turn up and I was roped in. I knocked him out in the 2nd round. But I could be sent anywhere to fight at almost a moment's notice. Chard... Gloucester... Shepton Mallet... Bridgwater... Cheltenham... You didn't even know who you were fighting. No such thing as contracts — and weights didn't matter. It wasn't unusual to end up taking on a bloke two stone heavier.

Jack Haskins (*left*) was the second row forward for Bristol and Gloucestershire. He was 6ft 4ins tall and '16½ stone of muscle, a mountain of a man'. Jack's two bouts with the rugged Kingsholm rugby player, Digger Morris, were engaging examples of the gimmicks dreamed up by Prince-Cox, the local promoter and Rovers boss.

Frank McElroy, who often boxed under the name of Young McAvoy and then Frank McAvoy, went on to become Southern Central welterweight champion. He vividly recalls his 'apprenticeship' days as a semi-pro, when he stepped through the ropes at Mangotsfield, Cheddar and the football ground at Swindon Town. Many West Country pundits had a high regard for him. 'But I was never in a position to train full-time. Boxing was, I suppose, a sort of hobby – frankly I wasn't enamoured at the idea of being knocked about!' Many patients at both Bath hospital and Frenchay have reason to be grateful for the work he did there as a remedial gymnast.

59

By the time I'd reached 30, I'd become a manager. I looked after Frank McAvoy and Jack Haskins. Frank did become Southern Central welterweight champion but I always felt he had the ability to go further. Jack, a fine rugby player, of course, was a great big mountain of a man without an ounce of fat on him. He was so big he could just push his opponents over. Prince-Cox had this great idea of putting one rugby man on against another, 'Digger' Morris, at Gloucester, a typical gimmick. Jack won, by the way.

Looking back on my own career, I feel I developed a 'sixth sense' with my left hand. But, of course, you didn't learn the trade at venues like Chard and Shepton Mallet — you needed to go to London. These days I'm happiest of all sitting at home listening to my Chopin and Beethoven records. Yet I can still nostalgically hear Fred Dyer's lovely Welsh voice... can still remember the suppers we were given after fighting as amateurs at the United Services Club in Narrow Wine Street or the Drill Hall... can still see Dad sitting in his corner seat at the Arcade, along with engine driver Bill Brewer, offering advice to the contestants! Oh dear, what warm memories...

Bristol bookmaker Bert Nutt, appointed an inspector for the Western area of the British Boxing Board of Control in recognition of his services to the sport, was once a boxer himself. He came from the Dings area of Bristol and, as a featherweight, used to fight as an amateur.

"I was only 16 when I went to Cirencester — to take part in an unlicensed show as a so-called pro. My opponent came from Stroud and he was a stone and a half heavier. He chased me all over the ring. I lost over six rounds — and got 15 bob for my pains.

"Gloucester's record-breaking Hal Bagwell was always topping the local bills in those days. What a remarkable lightweight he was — and, of course, his deeds are there in the Guinness Book of Records for everyone to read and wonder at. Just think of it. Unbeaten in 180 fights on the trot between 1938 and 1948. Some people weren't very impressed with the quality of the opposition in some of the war-time bouts. But just remember, he drew only five of those 180 contests.

"By comparison, I was a very modest performer in the ring. I used to fight as Bert McGrath, taking my mother's maiden name — and I remember they billed me as 'Gunner Nutt' at the Colston Hall in 1940. I was in the Royal Artillery at the time and really went along to the boxing show just to watch. My brother Jack was also home on leave and took on Billy White of Gloucester that night, losing on a cut eye. Well, Joe Pring's opponent didn't turn up. George Rose's brother, Reg, was the whip and he said to me: 'You're just the bloke.' On I goes... and I get a draw out of it.

"Everyone in this book has, I'm sure, talked of the great West Country characters around the boxing scene. I'll add two more names — Spud Murphy, from St. Philip's Marsh, who worked the booths like so many, and Bridgwater's Jack Marino. And I'm almost tempted to include the great George Rose in this category. How well I recall the way he trained us back at the old Dockland Settlement. He'd draw a circle on the floor. Then he'd kneel down with his hands behind his back — and challenge us to hit him. We simply couldn't. He was too damned clever. Do you know, when he sparred with Primo Carnero, George actually dived under his legs at one stage! A bit cocky if you like, but it brought a few laughs and loads of admiration."

Bert Nutt: boxer, army sgt-major, physical training instructor, bookmaker and BBBC area inspector. As a boy Bert won a Humane Society award for diving into the Feeder Canal and saving an 11 year-old from drowning.

Bert, a founder member of the West of England Sporting Club, also recalls a more poignant moment. "In 1951 I took Dixie Brown, by then blind of course, and another old-time booth fighter Bill Bridges to the Sugar Ray–Turpin contest at Earl's Court. Dixie was standing outside, a rather tragic looking figure, when Sugar Ray walked by. He paused — and then gave dear old Dixie a tenner."

From the Gem to the gallows

The fight game, back to the bareknuckle days, has often been touched by a whiff of scandal. Results have occasionally been rigged and the innuendos have even outnumbered the cheers. Boxers and their handlers have been known to tangle with the law. Flailing fists haven't always been limited to the ring.

Bristol, which has staged so many contests over the years, has probably had its share of tragic boxers — among them those who fell on hard times because they liked the Demon Drink perhaps rather too much or hadn't the resolve and self discipline to look after themselves properly to earn the rewards that their talents deserved.

This isn't the kind of book which dwells on misplaced dreams and mis-spent purses. We all have our sadder memories, however: of the Bristol champ who ended up sweeping the roads when he had every right to be basking in his fine reputation as a fighter; of the popular local lad who made such a poignant sight at the race-courses and football ground as he stood with his white stick and collecting box.

But that was part of the fabric of the sport, part of the sorry riddle of human nature. It all added to boxing's rich and flawed scenario. Could anything have been more dramatic and wretched, for instance, than the end of Del Fontaine... on the gallows?

He was a French Canadian but they loved him at Bristol's Gem. There was loads of action, not too much subtlety. He took plenty of punishment — and handed it out. The way he outpointed Red Pullen had the ringsiders on their feet. But Del (real name Raymond Henry Bousquet) was almost like a Bristol boy to them. Hadn't he fallen in love with a girl from Barton Hall?

Just three years after that all-action bout at the Gem, the girl, 21-year-old Hilda Meek was murdered in one of the country's most quoted contemporary crimes of passion. And the good-looking Del Fontaine was her killer.

The execution in London aroused much emotion. Fellow boxers joined the hundreds who gathered outside the prison. Hymns were sung and speeches against capital punishment were made. West Country friends added their names to the long list pleading for a reprieve. The recurrent question was: "Should a man suffering from acute depression and one who was probably punch-drunk have been

63

Del Fontaine – he ended in the condemned cell.

hanged?" At the trial, welterweight champion Ted Lewis was called for the defence. "At Del's last fight he shouldn't even have been allowed in the ring. Over the years he has received more punishment than any boxer I have ever known."

It was true that he was on the slide. After landing in England off a cattle boat in 1932 he had won all but four of his first 22 contests. By 1934 he was losing 12 out of 14. In the ring he looked dazed and confused.

Hilda Meek, born at Winstanley Street in Bristol, worked for a time as a waitress in a West End hotel. She talked of becoming a dancer. Clearly she was dazzled by the bright lights. And when Fontaine heard her making a date with another man, he pulled out a revolver and shot her as she ran into the street. He also wounded her mother with a second shot. Later he told police: "I spent my last cent on her. She broke me and ruined my health — and turned me against my own wife." Asked in court whether he realised that Fontaine had been knocked out seven times since his return from Canada, Hilda's bitter father said: "I don't know if they were knock-outs. The last one was a lie-down!"

In Canada, Del had known Bristol's Al Harding who persuaded him to fight at the Gem. Brother Percy was the promoter. A third brother, Terry Harding recalls: "He stayed at our home in The Cathay, Redcliffe. He was a likeable chap and made a great fuss of the kids. He was a good looking fellow with long black hair and a swarthy complexion. He was the first bloke I ever saw use after-shave!"

Al Harding cycled to London to visit him in the condemned cell. The dispirited prisoner pointed at the warders and said wryly: "They're looking after me all right, Al." It was the warders' turn to talk to Harding after the execution. "He was the bravest fellow we ever saw go to the scaffold."

Young Jimmy Cooper, aged 14.

The night a boy-fighter died

The last boxing promotion at the Gem Stadium, Broad Weir, Bristol, was on February 12th, 1934. It was also one of the most poignant evenings in the long history of West Country sport. Promising Jimmy Cooper, a "professional" for just six fights, collapsed and died in the ring. He was still a week short of his 15th birthday.

Jimmy's six-round bout with "Young Fear" was the first of the night. The stadium was buzzing with excitement as the two boxers, pale and wiry, climbed through the ropes. They traded punches and there was nothing between them at the end of the first round. Then, in the second, came tragedy. Young Cooper, urged on by his second and trainer, George Rose, was attacking strongly. But he suddenly retreated, appeared to slip and fell awkwardly with his chin resting on the canvas. Bob Wade, the referee, began to count and got to three. Jimmy half rose, put up his gloves in a token boxing attitude and collapsed in a heap.

Wade said later he saw Cooper changing colour. He gently lifted him to his corner, had a quick word with the second and the M.C. and declared the contest over. Dr. Frank Mogg, who was at the ringside, tried in vain to bring Cooper round; George Rose frantically rubbed the boy boxer's hands. Still unconscious, Jimmy was lifted from the ring and tenderly taken to a small room to await the ambulance. But he was already dead.

In the hall the crowd sensed that something was seriously wrong. They were very quiet, whispering to one another: "Is the lad all right?" George Perks, the M.C., came back into the main building and climbed onto a seat to address the spectators. "Ladies and gentlemen, I am sorry to announce that little Jimmy Cooper is gone. . . . "

The boy's father, Alfred, a familiar figure on crutches, kept repeating: "He's *not* dead, is he? Not dead. Not dead." George Rose buried his face in his hands to weep. The opponent, Gilbert Fare (Young Fear, as he was called on the billing) had the news broken to him as he sat morosely in the dressing room. He cried bitterly. Police arrived to take obligatory statements. The fight fans gradually drifted away, stunned and tearful. The distraught father was comforted and

BRISTOL BOY BOXER

Crowds numbering about 5,000 assembled outside the Dockland for the open-air service which preceded the interment in Avontery, Bristol, at yesterday's funeral of Jimmy Cooper, the four old Bristol boxer, who died in the ring last week. Below: Y who was matched with Jimmy Cooper in the tragic bout, and G the ... w ... graveside.

Vast crowds thronged the streets near the Dockland Settlement as the funeral cortege moves slowly past. The West Country has never seen a more moving farewell to a sporting figure.

IMPRESSIVE FUNERAL

taken home to Saxon's Yard, Church Street, St. Philip's, by the sister of the promoter Al Harding.

At the inquest, the verdict was that death had been caused from injuries "in a fall during a boxing contest". Medical evidence showed he had died from paralysis of the respiratory centre due to compression of the spinal cord by displacement of the 1st and 2nd vertebrae, caused by the fall.

Mr. Harding had told the inquest jury it was his fifth promotion at the Gem. Under cross-examination, he said they were not licensed but the premises were approved by the local authority. When it was the turn of Fare to give evidence, he said he understood that Cooper was 16 or 17. "After he went down, I stayed in my corner. Something seemed to tell me there was something wrong."

The two pairs of boxing gloves used in the contest were produced and examined. Various witnesses emphasised that it was a perfectly clean fight and there was no late punch from Fare once it was clear that Cooper was in trouble.

All eyes turned intently on the coroner, Mr. A. E. Barker, when he came to sum-up. There was no evidence at all of foul blows. But — and he weighed his words carefully and uttered them slowly — the jury might hold opinions "regarding the fact that the fight was not run under proper control auspices, such as the Boxing Board."

The funeral service was held on February 19th, a week after the tragedy. Seldom, if ever, has the city of Bristol witnessed a more moving occasion to pay respects to a single individual. Yet Jimmy Cooper was a humble 14-year-old lad who worked in a timber yard and fought on the occasional Monday night for a few bob a time.

Vast crowds lined the route along which the cortege passed on its way to Holy Trinity Church, St. Philip's. All seats were filled more than half-an-hour before the service. At least a thousand people gathered in the street outside. Six young Bristol boxers — Syd Elvins, Ted Makins, Tommy Bartlett, Billy Packer, Fred Gaydon and Pat Patterson — carried the coffin. Twenty-four boys from Barleyfields School, where Jimmy once attended, were present. The interment was at Greenbank Cemetery. After Jimmy's parents and the family, the countless friends filed tearfully past the grave. Many dropped little bunches of wild flowers onto the coffin. Tough, rugged boxers like George Rose had to be comforted.

That was the end of promotions at the Gem. The converted cinema would forever be associated with unhappiness and hints of guilt. Should a boy of 14 have been allowed to step into a ring with a young man of 22? It's a question that refuses to go away all these years later — though it should be remembered that Cooper was hardly a novice

The poignant graveside scene. George Rose (*in front*) is in tears. Jimmy opponent, 'Young Fear' is seen two to Rose's left. Among other well-known boxers in the silent group are Tommy Bartlett and Pat Patterson.

and looked well capable of taking care of himself in any ring. And, as everyone at the inquest agreed, "Young Fear" appeared in the box "a very small 22."

Dixie Brown was due to fight Bill Price at the Gem on the following week. That contest never took place. The doors were bolted. There were too many sad memories.

Working class Bristol had a generous heart in those days. Jimmy Cooper had been a popular figure at the Dockland Settlement. He was a good-living boy who went to church on Sundays and saved his violence for the ring. There was little money to spare within the family.

Burtwell Wigmore, the warden at the Dockland Settlement, launched an appeal. Immediately a group of unemployed in the building put their hands into almost empty pockets and raised seven shillings and tenpence. Local newspapers stirred a city's conscience. The wording on Mr. Wigmore's official appeal said: "Jimmy was a bright and promising boy, liked by all. His father, who is a cripple, is also a member of the senior club here — and his brothers are members, too. They are all very poor. Money will be needed

71

immediately, not to buy wreaths but to buy necessities." Albert Jennings started the fund with ten shillings. The Duke of Beaufort, who was a patron, sent a £1 note. There were collections in many of the local pubs and factories. Bristol Rovers forwarded £2.10s; the students at Wills Hall organised their own whip-round. The total reached £150.

We shall never know whether Jimmy Cooper, the boy boxer with his heart set on becoming a champ, would have lived up to the faith shown in him by his coach and mentor George Rose. Some said he lacked the lethal punch — just as the admired Rose did himself.

The memory of that fateful night at the Gem in 1934 continues to hover and haunt. Those pallid features and gamely flailing fists remain a poignant image to succeeding generations of West Country boxers and their supporters.

Jack Phelps — the voice of Bristol boxing

Jack Phelps is the authentic Voice of Bristol Boxing. He has been in his time trainer, second, manager, friend and confidant to many West Country fighters. No-one has more conscientiously researched and documented the careers of scores of local boxers, most of whom only dreamt of topping the bills. He had a kindly rapport with them, understanding the restrictions imposed by the poverty in which many of them grew up during the years of the Depression. He encouraged them to view boxing and physical fitness as a form of social therapy — and maybe a means for some to supplement breadline wages and a dole queue pittance. Jack chuckled over their earthy humour and, with loyal discretion, kept the more slanderous stories to himself. Never once did he lose his enthusiasm and affection for the sport.

He was born in the Whitehall district of Bristol and there was boxing in his blood. His father, a stud groom who looked after six horses at the Co-op stables, was also a lightweight booth fighter with personal experience of bareknuckle contests at Purdown. Jack was one of nine children — six girls and three boys — in a tight-knit family. But any hopes he cherished of becoming a boxer himself were cruelly dashed because of a tubercular condition affecting his right knee. He needed crutches for the first 10 years of his life and went on to have two major operations. "I'd have loved to be a champ" he confides. Instead, after starting work with a coal firm, he became a barber from the age of 20. High court judges, leading civic and sporting figures and members of the aristocracy were among his customers at Trowbridge's in Broad Street.

Physical culture emerged as something of a new fashion for boys and young men in the pre-war years. Jack believed in looking after the body and he started giving body-building lessons in his front room. His letter-headings and visiting cards referred to the Art of Self-Defence and advised potential pupils to "learn to box without punishment". He went on to operate from nine different gyms in the city. His first club was a room at the back of the Paxton Arms in Easton Road. Others included the Prince Albert, Two Mile Hill, while at the Rock Tavern, Olly Lodge, Speedwell, he had an improvised ring marked out on the cobbles. "I used to put down sawdust!"

But at a time when there were too many signs in working class Bristol of empty stomachs and hollow cheeks, Jack Phelps provided a sense of purpose for boys with no money and no job. He started his

Jack Phelps – carrying the big gloves and a head-ful of memories.

popular Speedwell Boxing Club in 1933. Three years later he took out a second's licence — and a manager's from 1938 right through to 1975 Today in his bachelor flat in a tower block overlooking Barton Hill, he remains sprightly; he never goes to bed without his obligatory 15 minutes of exercises, even though he is now in his mid-70s. His home is stacked with memories: cuttings, faded photographs, letters from ex-fighters. "Mr. Boxing", as he is known, will never be a lonely man.

❝❞ Yes, of course I'd have loved to be a boxer myself. The old knee stopped that but I never spared myself when it came to sparring. I'd take on six or seven, one after the other. I told the boys they could have a penny if they hit me on the nose, a shilling if they could make it bleed! But they never managed to hit me. My boxing was self-taught, in front of the mirror. I knew the third button on the waistcoat was the solar plexus. I watched the experts and read avidly. And I really did spar hundreds of rounds. Boxing had to be my life. And it still is.

I applied for my second's licence and it cost me five bob. All the kids I looked after were so game. You didn't throw the towel in. The manager's licence two years later set me back two guineas. So now, the obvious question is which of all the boxers I handled was the best. It has got to be Jimmy Jury, the mild-mannered taxi driver from Barnstaple. They say when he had a fare in the taxi he was an object lesson in charm and good manners. You should have seen him in a ring.

Jimmy was well known as a booth fighter for Sam McKeowen and I can still picture him performing on Horfield Common and Fish-ponds. He travelled all round the country with the booths and it was sometimes difficult to run him to ground. I used to get hold of him by sending a telegram c/o the fairground. Do you know, Jimmy invariably turned up, complete with his kit. He was always reliable. He had 21 fights in the four years I handled him and he nearly always came out clearly on top. A cool customer was Jimmy — he never wanted to know his opponent. Only the amount of the purse, and no-one could blame him for that!

Jury, who was to become West of England champion, fought as both a lightweight and welterweight. He really was an incredible bloke. He was so easy-going and calm in some respects. Before a fight, he'd go into the little dressing room and immediately fall asleep. We'd have to wake him and say: 'Come on, Jimmy, you're on!' He was one of the best body-punchers I ever saw. He would bang away at his opponents' ribs until all their strength had been sapped. Then he would go in for the knock-out punch.

75

There is no doubt in my mind that Jimmy was the cleverest boxer I looked after. But that brings me on to the inevitable follow-up. Who (and we're not going back to the days of Cribb, Gully and Belcher nor the best of the post-war boys like Terry Ratcliffe and Gordon Hazell) have been Bristol's finest boxers? I've spent hours weighing up their varied qualities, comparing one with another. No two local pundits will ever agree on the actual order.

Top of my list comes Harry Mansfield, from Bedminster. 'Fatty' Mansfield they called him, just because he claimed he liked to train for a fight on faggots and pies — and a pint or two of strong ale. The fact was that he was terrifically fit and had a wonderful defence. No-one could hit him. He made his opponents look sluggish. In the pubs around Bedminster, Harry was a great folk hero.

Like so many, he was a successful booth-fighter. He used to work Bill Moore's booth in the Horsefair — along with Mike Flynn and Chaffey Hayman. He also worked on the 'slogger' for Bill 'Sky' Lines. I never saw him in action, of course, but I read and heard so much about him. They used to say that he had the grace of a ballroom dancer in the ring and I can believe that. Between 1903 and 1906 he fought featherweight champion Jim Driscoll four times. And once he beat him over 10 rounds.

Harry didn't smile much. Once he climbed through the ropes he had a touch of arrogance about him. They said he didn't really like training — yet no-one ever criticised him for lack of stamina. He could sail through 20 rounds. His neighbours used to crowd into the Windmill Hill gym when he did his sparring. 'Fatty' was never more popular than when he took on the great Canadian featherweight George Dixon and drew with him in 1904. No wonder that the one-time heavyweight world champ Tommy Burns once tipped Harry for the top.

So why didn't he get there? He was simply badly guided, badly advised. Most of his fights were around the West Country and in Wales. Mansfield needed an imaginative, enterprising handler to point him in the right direction. Then there might have been no stopping him. Harry had for some years a job at the Waggon Works in Gloucester and some hinted that he lacked ambition himself. I find that very hard to believe and think it was a tragedy that he failed to command the fights — and the purses — that he deserved.

Nothing was more moving than the surprise visit to Bristol of Driscoll as Harry lay dying of consumption at his home in Philip Street. They exchanged memories and smiles of their four bouts. After the retired champion had gripped Harry's hand and said an emotional goodbye, the Bedminster man found a £5 note left under

Harry Mansfield.

Benny McNeill.

Jimmy Jury.

George Rose.

his pillow. There were so many examples of kind-heartedness in the boxing game.

Yes, I put Harry Mansfield first... narrowly. Second? Surely George Rose. He had a beautiful left hand and a quicksilver style. In fact, he had everything but a real punch. But he so often looked magnificent in the ring. At the Free Trade Hall, Manchester in 1930 he fought Al Foreman for the lightweight championship. It's true he lost in the sixth round but his strength had been sapped in trying to shed weight, at the last minute, for the contest. His purse for that championship bout — and his best — was £340. But I remember him telling me that he ended up with just £112.

George was my hero, no doubt about that. He used to lend me his 12-oz gloves on a Saturday night after being on the booths and I'd dutifully return them on the Monday. He was a very modest and popular man. I was very sad in the years when he fell on hard times. 'The only thing I've ever been able to do is box,' he once said to me. After he retired, still very much a local idol, he could have had a pub to run. 'But I didn't like the smell of beer,' he told me. In fact, he never drank and rarely if ever smoked.

In all he had 229 contests and lost 31. He beat every welterweight in the country and this stylish graduate from Barton Hill Boxing Club deserved far more rewards, in the material sense, than came his way. Latterly he was pushed around in a wheelchair. He died in 1978. Those of us who attended his funeral service, fellow boxers and friends from Bristol Rovers among the mourners, had a lump in our throats.

My No. 3 is Benny McNeill, the high-life featherweight from Fishponds. He had an undeniable taste for glamorous living. He made a relative fortune — and lost most of it. One could write a book about him alone. He went round the world. He made friends with millionaires and matched them in his generosity. Sadly he also went to jail.

In a much-publicised court case, he was charged with manslaughter after attacking his brother-in-law in a domestic wrangle. Benny went on the run, fearful of the consequences. I had many chats with him after his release from prison and he told me how he spent three nights sleeping rough on the Downs after committing the offence. He then crept to the home of George Harding, a member of the well-known butchery and boxing family, and was advised to give himself up.

I got to know him well and he never struck me as a violent person. He had a certain charm, plenty of personality and a voice which was full of Yankee colloquialisms that he had picked up during his career. 'At least they used to let me continue with my training while I was inside,' he'd tell me with that winning grin of his.

Benny fought in New York, Paris and London. The crowds liked him because of his attractive style in the ring. He had the voice of a Bristol boy and the manner of someone who had been around. There was never a problem getting him a fight. He earned at least £10,000 and that was really big money in the Twenties. For my money he was an all-round boxer. It wasn't surprising that Ted Broadribb managed him for a time. McNeill, 'the fighting machine' had an imposing list of illustrious victims.

There was something sad about him by the time he had his last fight, back at Bedminster's Arcade Hall, against Ginger Britton. The old fire and swagger had gone. It was hard to realise that this was the boxer who once refused to meet Jim Driscoll in Bristol — because the purse wasn't big enough! But having said that, Benny could be terrifically generous. If someone complimented him on his suit, he'd reply: 'You can have it.' And he meant it.

Before I complete my list of personal favourites I must mention Alf Avent and Dixie Brown — even though Alf was well before my time and Dixie came from the West Indies. Avent wasn't very big but everyone is agreed that he was very good indeed. Just before the turn of the century, this Bedminster boy won the amateur bantamweight championship. And it took nearly 60 years before another local fighter, Terry Ratcliffe, was able to reach the same high level at welterweight.

Alf's brother, Frank, who lived to the age of 91, was flyweight champ of the West of England. He was stopped by the great Jimmy Wilde in 1911 and also pulled in the Bristol fans when he fought an exhibition bout with Wilde on the stage of the Empire, Old Market.

Dixie arrived in Bristol from Cardiff at the age of eight. His name was George Charles. He was everybody's friend, amiable, good-natured... and desperately unlucky. He lost his sight and life drifted away tragically for him. Certainly he was a victim of the colour bar and as such failed to receive the official acclaim and recognition that his neat ring style warranted.

George Perks was a fine judge of a contestant and rated Dixie highly as a box-fighter. True Dixie liked a drink and wasn't always surrounded by the best-intentioned of company. Not once did he short-change a crowd. We shall never be too sure how many fights he actually had; some in the smaller venues simply weren't recorded. It is true that he lost almost as many bouts as he won. That shouldn't reflect a lack of ability — it meant, rather, that he was matched too often against unsuitable opponents. When a controversial verdict went against him, as it was apt to do, he shrugged those smooth, ebony shoulders and said to his second: 'When's the next fight?'

His final contest was against Jack Lewis at the Colston Hall. By then his sight was so blurred that he was forced to give up. His long-time handler George Harding shook his head sadly. The crowd were embarrassed and sympathetic. For three or four years he'd been boxing virtually blind in one eye. Now everyone realised it had to end. 'Poor old Dixie — what can he do now?' people asked. A warm-hearted well wisher sent him to Vienna to see a leading eye specialist. The operation wasn't a success.

Bristol's boxing public didn't lack compassion. A collection from the ring raised £60 (a similar one for George Rose surprisingly brought in only £29). Friends continued to buy him a drink or occasionally drop a florin into his breast pocket. He was dead by the age of 56.

I retain many warm memories of Dixie. One is of one Sunday morning after he'd lost his sight. Prince-Cox sent me to Dixie's home in Knowle West to persuade him to come back with me and appear on the stage of the Empire that evening in one of the popular In Town Tonights. He agreed eventually. A packed auditorium rose quite emotionally to him as he stumbled on with his white stick, guided by me. An appeal was made on his behalf and he left the Empire that night with tears in his eyes. His pockets were stuffed with pound and ten shilling notes from friends and admirers.

St. Lucia never sent a more engaging man to this country. There are many still around who remember Dixie doing his stuff on the booths — just as they remember his memorable contest with George Rose at the Colston Hall. He lost on points over 15 rounds. But that really was a fight to cherish.

Where do I stop in this nostalgic roll of honour? There must be a place for Reg Hall and Jack Dale, for Fred Gaydon and Ginger Britton, Len Munden and Frank McAvoy . . . there is a score of other names rushing into my head, all of them courageous, capable West Country boys who pounded away for a few quid and hopes of elusive glory. Talking of McAvoy, I have recently found a typical 'challenge' from the papers of those days:

YOUNG McAVOY WILL BOX ANY BOY IN THE WEST OF ENGLAND AT 8 STONE, GIVE OR TAKE 2 LBS. JACK PHELPS IS CONFIDENT THAT McAVOY IS A FUTURE FLYWEIGHT CHAMPION OF THE WEST. HE WOULD LIKE TO MEET EITHER REGGIE HALL OR TIGER POMPHREY.

Top: Coalman 'Honest Joe' Pring, the first boxer Jack Phelps managed (Joe was topping the bill at the Winter Gardens, Weston as late as 1952), and Dixie Brown (*right*) a great favourite though sadly at times a victim of the colour bar.

Bottom: Another era . . . another batch of boxing hopefuls. Mentor Phelps sits with them, still passing on advice, at the Empire Club in Bristol. The successes of young Darren Thompson, one of his pupils, gave him great pleasure. Darren, son of Alan Thompson, an outstanding schoolboy boxer, was junior ABA champion in 1982 – 'my first champion', says Jack proudly.

Or, as an intriguing alternative:

GEORGE BRYANT, NOW IN FULL TRAINING AGAIN, WOULD
LIKE TO TRY CONCLUSIONS WITH ANY BOY IN THE WEST,
ARNOLD ROSE PREFERRED, OVER TEN ROUNDS.

I wrote above of Jack Dale. He was a stylish and useful local boxer. Do you know that when he beat Phil Clements on points in a winner-take-all bout at the Drill Hall, Old Market in 1925, he discovered that the Gloucester man was broke. His immediate reaction was to insist on paying Clements' fare home. Just another instance of the camaraderie of the Twenties and Thirties.

Perhaps I should add two more accolades to my earlier list. For my money Albert Jennings was the best referee and Bob Wade the best teacher. I don't think too many people, intimately connected with the sport in the pre-war days, will disagree with my assessment.

There was so much courage then, too. Young boxers took a pasting, shrugged off their bruises and were back at work early next morning — that was if they were lucky enough to have a job. When it comes to sheer courage, I always tell people of that extraordinary scrap at the Bedminster Arcade between Charlie Little and Alfie Ovens. It was all-action from start to finish. Both of them kept slugging away and taking so much punishment. At one stage they slumped on to the canvas together — and somehow staggered on to their feet again.

And, of course, no-one could really top Tiger Pomphrey for guts. He took so much and kept coming back for more. Tiger always gave the crowd their money's worth. He may have lacked a bit of finesse and the art of defence. But what a great battler he was. The trouble was he used to hit with the inside of the gloves, which meant he wasn't scoring.

Joe Pring from Knowle West was the very first boxer I managed. He was such a sincere chap that I dubbed him 'Honest Joe'. I suppose I had something of a flair for publicity. Many young boxers used to fight under a different name — to hoodwink the Labour Exchange. But I was apt to change the names of a few others, to give them more of a boxing image. Frank McElroy became Frank McAvoy, for instance, when I managed him. And I billed Freddie Cooper as 'Young Rose' because he had good footwork which reminded me of George.

Management gave me one or two headaches, even though I admit I was perhaps never in the Jack Solomons class! I had a boxer called Charlie Davis, a stonemason from Staple Hill. It looked in 1938 as though he might have a modestly useful career ahead of him. He was

82

confident enough to buy a new kit for himself. But then, just three days before a scheduled fight at the Colston Hall, he cried off. Just like that. 'I've finished with boxing, Jack. Sorry.'

Prince-Cox, the promoter, was livid. He blamed me rather than Charlie. I tried to get to work on his father, Danno Davis, and sister, who couldn't understand why this promising boxer had suddenly packed it in. All to no avail. Charlie never once put the gloves on again. Don't ask me why — although I did hear that he'd started courting!

As a manager I had one brief brush with the British Board of Control, also in 1938. It was at the time Charles 'Dolly' Roberts bought the Magnet cinema in Newfoundland Road and planned to turn it into a boxing arena. He installed a full-size ring; he bought the gloves and most of the necessary equipment. Mr. Roberts, a successful fish shop proprietor (not to mention inventor and man of boundless ideas), decided to bring me in as his partner and adviser. But sadly not a single fight was ever staged there. I got suspended by the Board and I'm still trying to work out why. Officially it was over the 10 per cent they claimed I took from my boxers' fight fee. But they didn't seem to realise how I cushioned my boys, paying for their boots, gum shields and never charging a training fee. Looking back on it, the Board's attitude was to me heavy-handed and pretty unfair. I felt the local boxing establishment ganged up on me.

Maybe I should have a passing word about the booth fighters — after all, my father was briefly one. Opinions vary about their worth and, of course, their genuineness. I can only speak nostalgically. Whether at Bridgwater Fair or Horfield Common, they were a colourful and invariably entertaining and popular facet of the travelling shows.

Yes, we know there were some good-natured fiddles and the booth boxers seldom lost. Just ask some of the survivors about the famous gee-fights, as they were called. It was after all part of showbiz. The bouts needed an element of exaggerated presentation and a few phoney claims. When I hear people knocking the old booth fights and saying it was all a sham, I remind them how valuable they were to the pros who took part. It kept them in trim and practice — and provided some useful, if hard earned, pocket money, too. Just think of the many fine fighters who started on the booths, Freddie Mills, Benny Lynch and the Turpins among them. The booths were the best school in the world and I think it was a mistake when they got banned.

I love the fight game. The majority of the fighters are delightful blokes — and I'm not forgetting the few who couldn't cope with success, who liked a drink too much and who couldn't keep away from

Best wishes
Jack Phelps
1934

Above: Jack Phelps, posed professionally for the sport he would in his heart have loved to follow as a boxer, rather than trainer and manager.

Below: Bob Wade, 'the best teacher of young boxers I ever knew'. He had gone into the Royal Navy at the age of 18 and was a successful boxer himself in the Services. His various schools of boxing (or academies as they were sometimes called) were famous in the Bristol area. He also built up a sound reputation as a referee. Bob lost a foot in the Bristol blitz when serving as an air raid warden.

the women. Do you know, it struck me time and again that many boxers held a fatal fascination for the ladies!

I have attended the funerals of a great number of Bristol and West of England boxers, some of whom had fallen into bad company and blown what money their fists had earned them in the ring. There were tears unashamedly in my eyes at the graveside. I still hear from their families and I'm proud of those warm associations. There's a lovely sentimentality and goodwill about boxing that you don't get in many other sports.

We have so many to thank for the vibrant history of boxing in the socially difficult days of the Twenties and Thirties, the period about which this book is mainly devoted. I think back to marvellous names like Bob Wade and Bert Budd; to Charlie Hobbs who encouraged that thriving enthusiasm centred on the old Beer Cask pub; to Albert Jennings; to old local boxing families like the Hardings and the Coopers, the Locks, the Halls, the Tites and the Bessells and many more; to those who worked tirelessly to ensure the success of the fight game at places like Weston, Bath, Yeovil, Bridgwater and Gloucester. And I think of respected coaches like my good friend Billy Walker who died in 1987. This one-time exponent at the fairground booths later had a great influence on boxing at the Dockland Settlement and then the Empire Club.

What days! What wonderful scraps! What characters! I feel I've known them all. Coached them as boys, crouched in their corners, cheered at their successes. They weren't all champs by any means. But most of them had something in common. They were HUNGRY FIGHTERS. An empty belly was the greatest motivation of all and it isn't any accident that many of the finest boxers of all times grew up from extreme poverty.

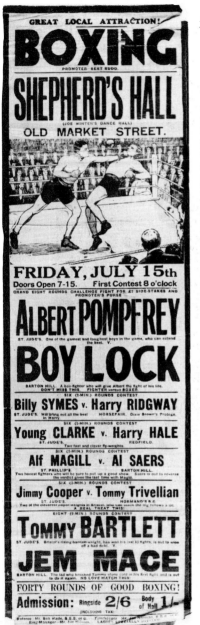

Poster Power

This is a typical 'all-action' bill of the period: crammed with local names and, in this case, carrying a modest £2 side-stake on the top contest. Other posters have their own quaint and appealing phraseology. For Tommy Bartlett's 10-rounder with hard-hitting Jack Ellis, from Plymouth, at the Gem, the intriguing question is posed 'Who will kiss the canvas first?' In a contest featuring Tiger Pomphrey, we are told reasonably enough: 'Patrons can rest assured of seeing a real good slam.' And when George Rose tops the bill at the Barton Hill Baths, his opponent for the 15-round battle, Bristol's Bill Price is described as 'The City's Coming Welterweight Spoiler of Champions'. The Bert Budd promotions often made it clear that 'ladies are specially invited'. Occasionally an opponent's name is left blank but potential customers are promised: 'Other contests, time permitting'. There is no question of being short-changed on an evening's entertainment. The spectrum of local names reflects the collective sense of pugilistic ambition – if not the need for a few extra bob. Taunton's Albert Paddick and Bristolians Reg Evans, Stan Hall, George Bryant, Tommy Coles, Len Cottle, George Hillier and Alf Dwyer are names plucked at random from early bills at Shepherd's Hall, the Gem and Barton Hill Baths.

Jem Mace, from Barton Hill, is challengingly billed as 'the lad who knocked Tommy Bartlett stone cold and is out to do it again – no love match this!' As for Frome's Eric Cheston, he is 'the gentleman boxer who likes it'. The Red Triangle Hall, Farrington Gurney staged a number of shows in the early 30s. Dixie Brown turned up for a four-round exhibition with Jack Harvey, 'the fighting blacksmith from Stanton Drew'. Clearly there was plenty of local support for Paulton's George Norris, Pensford's Sonny Hellier and 'Young Minall' of Clutton. Their opponents included the likes of 'Battling Ford, of South Bristol'. The referees ranged from Bert Budd to Bombardier Billy Wells. George Perks, with those distinctive arm gestures and the wafting voice, was often the MC. He was also inclined to take an advert in the programme, claiming to give the best haircut in Bristol for sixpence 'at 42, Bridge Street, first floor'.

Few matched 'Tiger' Pomphrey when it came to raw courage. He took untold punishment and kept coming back – to the delight of every West Country crowd. Here he is as an 18 year-old. There were so many brave local boxers – like Southville's Fred Tite who memorably, after breaking his jaw in the 3rd round at the Arcade Hall, still matched Welshman Ivor Jones punch-for-punch. Fred was something of an idol in Bedminster during the Thirties. In all he had 250 fights, beat Fred Gaydon three times (no mean achievement) and appeared on the first professional bill at the Colston Hall, defeating Len Balley, of Bath.

Stan 'Billy' Williams (*left*), who came from Kingswood, was apt to be billed as 'the fighting Sunday School teacher'. In fact, he was a keen worker for the local community and served as a youth club leader in Kingswood for a time. A popular boxer, he had 14 contests as an amateur and 85 as a pro. It's true he lost in the 2nd round to George Rose but he went 15 rounds and drew with Jack Dale. It used to be said that this likeable boxer used a different name in the ring so that people wouldn't pick on him in the street! Teddie Makins (*right*), whose home was at Shirehampton, was a promising bantamweight. But he lost his life at sea in the last war.

Above: Billy Wagner, talented West middleweight champ who went on to manage Hal Bagwell. Left: Eddie Norton was a very capable boxer in his own right and the welterweight West of England title-holder. Later he promoted regularly at the Bedminster Arcade and also refereed.

Above: Freddie Cooper, younger brother of the tragic Jimmy, is seen with some of his trophies. They dubbed him 'Young Rose' because his footwork reminded them at times of George.

Right: The serviceman is Alfie Ovens, a gritty local boxer who never knew when he was beaten.

Tommy Ingleton, real name Harry Incledon (*left*) was a popular Bedminster-born welterweight, who had his first organised fight against his school chum George Carey at a flower show in Bristol. "I was about eleven at the time and we had three 1½ minute rounds!" he recalls. This former choirboy took the name 'Tommy' from his uncle. He had something like 35 professional bouts, mostly in the locality, and impressed the crowds with his attacking style and his gameness. He started work as a junior office boy and later worked for the Co-op, in the stables and bakery department. But he was for many years until his retirement a member of the Fire Service, being a Sub-Officer at both Weston-super-Mare and Bridgwater. He's now in his late 70s and lives at Highbridge. Phil Green (*right*), a Midlander who lived in Bath, was the middleweight champion of the West and is seen here wearing the belt. He was a modest, capable boxer who was matched against Jock McAvoy and boxers of that calibre. Phil had a magnificent physique in the ring – and, like so many, a gentle manner out of it.

Danny Regan was a tough and loquacious Irishman, who was apt to acquire friends and run into spots of trouble. An ex-army champion, he came to Bristol and lodged over an ice-cream parlour in Milk Street. He took part in a particularly lively contest – and eventually lost – with Tom Ind at the Drill Hall, Old Market.

Charlie Davis was the Staple Hill stonemason who told his manager, Jack Phelps; 'Sorry, I've had enough of boxing'.

A marvellous, expressive (and rare) shot of the Fighting Pomphrey Brothers – George, Albert (Tiger), and Arthur.

Three of Bristol's best get together for a stream of reminiscences. Middleweight Gordon Hazell, welterweight George Rose (not long before his death) and another welterweight Terry Ratcliffe.

Index